GRIMOIRE
GIRL

Also by
Hilarie Burton Morgan

The Rural Diaries

GRIMOIRE GIRL

Creating an Inheritance
of Magic and Mischief

HILARIE BURTON MORGAN

HarperOne

An Imprint of HarperCollinsPublishers

Pages 60, 187: "Figs from Thistles: First Fig" and "Witch-Wife" Copyright © 1956 by Norma Millay Ellis from *Collected Poems* by Edna St. Vincent Millay, published by Harper & Brothers Publishers.

Page 62: "[i carry your heart with me(i carry it in]" Copyright © 1952, 1980, 1991 by the Trustees for the E. E. Cummings Trust, from *Complete Poems: 1904–1962* by E. E. Cummings, edited by George J. Firmage. Used by permission of Liveright Publishing.

Page 63: "Within a Flower" from *The Poems of Emily Dickinson*, edited by Thomas H. Johnson, Cambridge, Mass.: The Belknap Press of Harvard Univ. Press, Copyright © 1951, 1955 by the President and Fellows of Harvard College.

Pages 84–85: Meyer Lemon and Blood Orange Shrub Recipe from *Blotto Botany* by Spencre L. R. McGowan (New York: HarperCollins Publishers, 2018) used by permission of the publisher.

Pages 102, 185: C. P. Cavafy, "The City" from *C. P. Cavafy: Collected Poems*. Translated by Edmund Keeley and Philip Sherrard. Translation Copyright © 1975, 1992 by Edmund Keeley and Philip Sherrard. Reproduced with permission of Princeton Univ. Press.

Page 178: Kennedy-Cairns, Lulu. "To Sir With Love." 1967 performance. Written by Don Black and Mark London, lyrics used with permission of Screen Gems/EMI Music.

FIRST EDITION

Designed by Nancy Singer

Background on pages i, 7–12, 19–22, 30–33, 48–51, 59–64, 72–78, 92–99, 107–109, 122–129, 142–145, 167–171, 179–183, 192–195, 201–204, 219–220 © Nimaxs/Shutterstock

Background on pages ii–iii, xiv–1, 79, 146–147 and "Simple Spells" potion bottle © Wonder studio/stock.adobe.com

Hands on page iii © Maria Zamchiy/stock.adobe.com

Hands on pages 1, 79, 147 and chapter opener/part opener crystal balls © Ксения Хомякова/stock.adobe.com

Illustrations on pages 2, 14, 24, 34, 52, 66, 80, 100, 110, 130, 148, 172, 184, 196, 206, 220 © Olivia Faust

Ouroboros on pages 13, 23, 65, 205 © Kovaltol/Shutterstock

Library of Congress Cataloging-in-Publication Data has been applied for.

ISBN 978-0-06-322273-1

23 24 25 26 27 LBC 5 4 3 2 1

To my rosebud, George.
My magical boy, Gus.
My Jeffrey.

"They are the we of me."

—*Carson McCullers*

CONTENTS

Preface   ix

I. The Past Is Present

✦

1. Inheritance   3

Simple Spells: Tools to Start Your Own Grimoire 7

2. Name Your Home   15

Simple Spells: We Are Water 18

3. Ithaca   25

Simple Spells: Altars 30

4. Fountain of Youth   35

Simple Spells: Talismans for Your Rebellion 48

5. Storytelling   53

Simple Spells: Poetry Spells 59

6. No Beige Homes   67

Simple Spells: Candle Magic 72

II. Into a Dark Wood

✦

7. Making Friends with Ghosts   81
Simple Spells: Parties and Potions 92

8. Paper Mail   101
Simple Spells: The Art of Letter Writing 107

9. The Coven You Keep   111
Simple Spells: Celestial Bodies 122

10. Synchronicities   131
Simple Spells: Write Your Own Eulogy 142

III. Returning Home

✦

11. Look to Antiquity   149
Simple Spells: Goddesses, Gods, Saints, and Such 167

12. Flower Power   173
Simple Spells: Secret Language of Flowers 179

13. Find Your Muse   185
Simple Spells: Make Your Own Oracle Deck 192

14. Enchanting Your Food   197
Simple Spells: Sweet Hot Pot Pie 201

15. Giving It Away   207
Simple Spells: Ithaka 219

Afterword 221
Acknowledgments 224

PREFACE

I have been fascinated with the idea of a grimoire since I was very little. As a kid, grimoires were fearsome things that excited my curiosity. Witches kept them, accumulating magic so rare and dangerous that secrecy became paramount. But there was a catch: anything witch-oriented was banned in our home. No Smurfs and their meddling magic. The movie *Bedknobs and Broomsticks* got me in a heap of trouble for chanting, "Treguna mekoides trecorum satis dee!" around the house. And Ouija boards were for those courting the devil.

I really don't think it was that our home was deeply invested in the hysterical Satanic Panic of the 1980s. But I do think my elders were abundantly cautious. *Why meddle with the unexplained?*

I wasn't very good at following the rules, though. And I started keeping my own tiny versions of grimoires. Journals under my bed, books of depressing and sentimental poetry that I'd picked up here and there, scrapbooks made from magazine cutouts and ticket stubs, and newspaper articles.

I wanted to record and keep and collect, an innate habit that grew and grew well into my young adulthood. Then, when I had children? Good lord, I felt an even deeper desire to catalogue life. I wanted to make it make sense for them. But that meant wading through so much of my own bullshit first. What was important to me? Which parts of my life were worth keeping and which were old phases meant to be discarded? What did I want my kids to know about me? Or their father, or any of our other loved ones?

When we typically think of a grimoire, we picture witches harboring secrets. We think of that book with the fantastic eye in the movie *Hocus Pocus* that Bette Midler uses to conjure evil spells. We think of mysterious texts, purchased in back-alley stores and passed down through generations. And that's really not so far-fetched. Have I bought some questionable ancient books from seedy bookstores? Affirmative. Have I passed down family practices that venture into mystical territory? Proudly.

Self-identifying as a witch is an act of rebellion. And a grimoire is a testament to your power and your craft.

Writing knowledge down so that it does not become lost was once a highly dangerous practice for women. How many stories have we heard about women in fourteenth- and fifteenth-century Europe being tortured, burned, or hanged for their independence and wisdom? Every school kid in America has learned about the savagery of the Salem Witch Trials. A found grimoire could be a death sentence, and so these books were not frivolous creations kept for sentimental purposes.

A grimoire was a guide to *keep you alive*.

It held knowledge about plants—which ones would save your life and which would kill you. It contained ceremonies and rituals believed to honor God, or gods and goddesses. It was the tangible collection of a lifetime of learning. A woman would record what she'd been taught as a child and add to it throughout her lifetime. The fairer sex would learn from each other and cautiously trade remedies. To be imprinted in another woman's grimoire was an act of trust—from both parties.

Once my daughter, George, was born, I started collecting scraps of information, quotes, book excerpts, and other pieces of knowledge in a leather-bound journal with creamy thick pages and irregular edges. A grimoire of ideas and habits I wanted her to have.

The idea of inheritance was important to me. As I looked into her little rosebud face, I struggled to find what I could give her and my son, Gus, that would outlast me. The thing I wanted to leave my children was joy. Secrets. Curiosity. Mischief. I wanted them to have a sense of self that would be a strong canvas on which they could add their own splashes of color and narrative.

The moment I started working on it, a global catastrophe took over, and suddenly we were all collectively examining our own mortality. Life sure has a way of kicking you square in the ass, doesn't it? Big questions loomed for all of us. Who are we in the absence of office culture and without packed calendars of parties or dates or kids' soccer games? What does this mortal coil hold, if it's not dressed up in fashion or uniforms?

Well, all that did was make me even more motivated to commit pen to paper and record these musings. And now it wasn't just for my children, but as a reminder for myself. There were dark days in there, friends. I don't know anyone who emerged from lockdown unscathed. We either grew too hard or too soft or too embittered or painfully empathetic. I struggled with how to ground myself, to remember the healthy practices or creative habits that brought me joy. I didn't want my kids—who were home more than ever at that point—to look back on the lost years and remember their mom as a shell of a woman. I also didn't want them thinking I was a faker. So that tender balance between admitting that life is hard and seeking out the good in it became the tightrope I walked on a daily basis.

Then we started emerging from our pandemic cocoons and venturing out. Things were looking up, right? My husband, Jeffrey, and I took our kids on a vacation to Sagamore Beach in Massachusetts. The tiny house we rented was a time capsule of simpler times. The bedroom was just large enough to fit a double bed with room around it to shimmy sideways. The wood-paneled walls displayed pictures of the owners' grandma in her rocking chair. The actual rocking chair sat right below. The guestbook was a log preserving a decade of visits from close family members, recounting lunches with uncles and cousins' birthdays and bioluminescence in the water. It seemed the owners only opened the house up to strangers when the world shut down and people were desperate for coastal hideaways. Ours was one of the very few non-family entries recorded, making us feel special, like long-lost distant cousins.

Our last night there, I saw two shooting stars. I'd never seen a shooting star before. There were always meteor showers in Wilmington, North Carolina, when I lived there, but I'll level with you—I always lied about being able to see them. I figured I just had bad eyes. Or I wasn't patient enough to stare up at the sky to catch them. But in truth, all those previous stars were not for me. They were meant for other people to see.

So, I'd fib. "Oh wow," I'd muse along with everyone else. "That was wild." But on that one night in early August 2021, I saw two of them. And it was indeed wild. The next day, on our drive home I found out my Christmas-movie mom Markie Post had left us. Nine days later, one of my most beloved friends, Willie Garson, told us he was stopping treatment for cancer.

I sat on planes. I sat at bedsides. I sat at memorials. I sat posted up at home on my phone, texting with the bereaved. I sat alone at my computer, watching videos of these powerfully alive humans. Willie would pass a few short weeks later.

As I sit here working on this grimoire, I remind myself to be grateful for what my friends gave me. Intangible gifts that seeped deeply into my identity. I will integrate them into my own hodgepodge of inheritance. I will insert them—and the gifts from others I've loved and lost—into my grimoire. My children will have these things. Ideas and habits and traditions passed down, not knowing where my friends' influence stops and I begin. It will have all melded into something they can expand upon.

So anyway, all of that is to say that this isn't a morbid book about loss. This is my grimoire. My own personal collection of rituals and practices and beliefs and knowledge. As the pieces came together, I started to see the threads of a journey I've been on: a quest that led me through a dark wood and delivered me to a new understanding of home, full of magic I'd accumulated along the way.

Home is the cornerstone of magic, after all. It is safety. It is comfort. It is sacred and divine. Like the grimoires of old, full of life-saving wisdom, these pages contain the things that have kept me alive: people, places, stories. And because I want to share things that can infuse magic into your daily life, it also will include what I'm calling *Simple Spells*, where you can dive into crafting an altar, using poetry spells, flower magic, and the realization that you've already been practicing magic all along.

Hopefully these pages will be an inspiration for you to create your own grimoire, your personal source of everyday enchantment. This is a book about living so hard and with so much intention that your people see the shooting star in you. Let's burn bright.

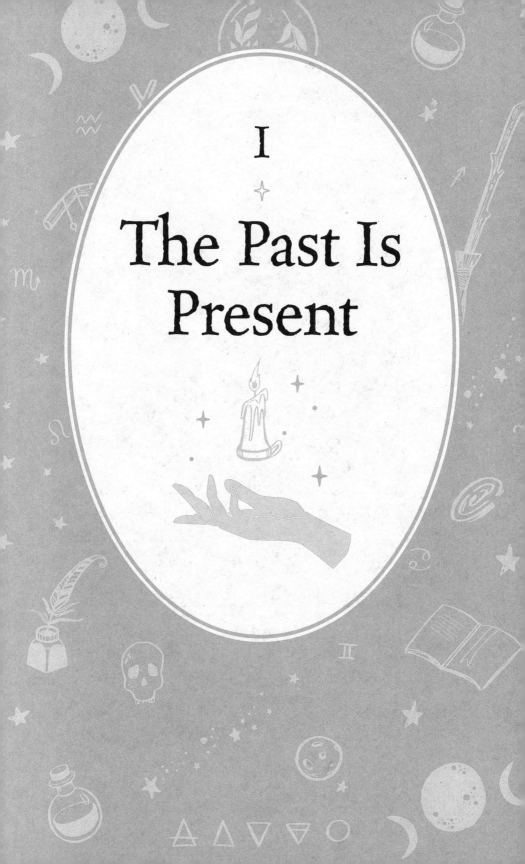

I

The Past Is Present

INHERITANCE

What will my children inherit from me?

Inheritance. I just marvel at that.

Not because I'm an orphan or an island. But I didn't come from a connected family. It's not my place to talk about the decisions my parents made with their own relatives; we all have our reasons for moving along with the tides of personal growth. That said, I haven't spent meaningful time with either side of my family in almost thirty years. I'm okay with that. There are second cousins and distant relatives I've connected with on social media. And while we don't know each other all that well, I see the noble lives they live and the kindness they strive to put into the world. This commonality between us feels good as we digitally wave to each other from across the country.

But there were no sleepovers.

No secrets shared.

No big table of beaming relatives at my wedding. My whole life,

I've heard stories about my friends' families. Mischievous cousins and eccentric aunts and uncles and cuddly grandparents and mystical great-grandparents. I'd insert myself into these families, calling other people's relatives Grammy and Papa. I adopted high school teachers as surrogate elders. I made cousins of my girlfriends and beloved coworkers. I didn't have ancestors passing along traditions and knowledge, so I curated my own blend of appointed ancestors along the way and collected the knowledge they gifted me.

I wanted a story of my own. A family tree that spread out like an ancient live oak, its branches sweeping and accessible. A family tree you could climb and touch, rough bark against your palms and vivid greenery against your cheek. So, it makes sense that as a kid, I was always hungry to know more. And since I didn't have relatives to share their stories with me, I turned to my surroundings to fill in the details, stealing scraps of information while trying to paint a picture of the family I didn't know.

I sat at the feet of my parents as they gossiped and shared stories with other adults. I clocked every inference, every reference to my history. Eavesdropping was my *jam*. But the physical evidence of our lineage hid, divided between an ornate credenza in our dining room and a tall, ebony-stained secretary desk in our living room.

These were my cookie jars to pilfer.

Poised and nonchalant, I'd position myself close to these treasure chests of information, waiting for my parents to leave. Once I'd hear the aluminum screen door close, I'd begin my excavation.

The drawers were creaky and loud, stuffed with the paper trail of a lifetime that predated my consciousness. There were yellowing photographs of people I never knew. Pictures of me as a wispy-haired baby on the laps of strangers. There were titles to cars we no longer owned and receipts for the furniture that was now threadbare, torn apart by an army of Burton toddlers. Especially surprising were incriminating pictures of my parents with friends and beer bottles, two things they never kept in the house anymore. My father would take scraps of paper—sometimes the backs of billing envelopes with their crinkly cellophane windows, sometimes restaurant napkins—and in his slanted, angular handwriting record hilarious things my brothers had said. Humor to be remembered for all of posterity.

Key chains. Matchbooks. An old chunky glass ashtray. Ziploc bags full of clippings from first haircuts. Baby teeth. A small leather address book that was brought out once a year to send Christmas cards.

This, I pored over.

This, I memorized.

This, I embellished into a full family portrait.

The junk drawers were my inheritance.

After Jeff and I moved our family to our farm in the winter of 2014, my dad made a trip with a U-Haul full of furniture. The dining room set that had been a wedding gift to my parents was mine now. The table with oak veneer peeling off in corners, and chairs that had grown wiggly by unruly kid butts, we moved in the entire suite piece by piece.

The credenza was also now mine, but it was empty.

Fuck.

It makes me tear up to write that all these years later.

The magical, mysterious credenza that I was so certain held the pieces to a lineage I was desperate to puzzle together was barren. Was this one of those metaphors I was supposed to recognize in real time? I didn't. I was still greedy for artifacts.

None of my brothers had wanted any of the family china, so I took it all. The set was a mishmash of gold-trimmed Nippon that had been scoured from flea markets up in the Appalachian Mountains and junk shops of my native Virginia and salt and pepper shakers passed down from my Dutch relatives in the Midwest. At long last, my great-great-grandparents' wedding teacups were mine, their pastel blue and pink flowers fading into obscurity but not totally gone. I could squint and blur my vision to make out the outlines of vague petals, imagine what they looked like without the cracks and yellowing of time.

They were mine.

And yet I still didn't know any more about my history, about who I was and where I came from, than I did as a kid rummaging through the drawers of forbidden furniture. Without a story passed down to me, it was up to me to write my own story. To take the mismatched china, the chipped dining table, the empty credenza, and fill them in with the memories of my childhood, crafting an inheritance for myself.

And not just for myself. I started to wonder: How do I play an active role in crafting my children's inheritance while I'm still very much here? I want to be aware of what I'm living and creating in the moment. And I want to leave them with behaviors, traditions, funny habits, and a sense of curiosity that outweighs any material inheritance. Because while I treasure the things that have been passed down to me, never have I seen *things* listed in a memorial or obituary. Ownership is not a legacy! People leave behind loved ones, passion projects, traditions.

When I call it, what are they gonna write about me?

This crazy old bat believed in aliens and Bigfoot, lived in more than a couple of haunted houses, had crystals and seashells all over her home, wrote thousands of paper letters, talked to plants, knew a little magic, could curse a blue streak, and worshipped her children.

If our lives are our greatest art projects, let's get to crafting.

Tools to Start Your Own Grimoire

Writing itself was a magical act in which imagination altered reality and gave form to power.

—Alice Hoffman, *Rules of Magic*

*L*et's begin.

If we are to collect all our life-saving knowledge and the secrets of our hearts, we need a vessel. For me, what started out as marble composition notebooks in middle school grew into a vast collection of velvet- and leather-bound journals. Each chapter of my life has produced a separate grimoire, if for no other reason than I am addicted to beautiful blank books, full of promise and potential. The combination of all of those texts has been handwritten into a large bundle of handmade paper—with raw edges, bound in a buttery soft leather. It is the kind of creation that makes me want to be intentional with every marking I make on its pages. If you are searching for your perfect grimoire, consider sketchbooks. I love that they refuse the structure of lines and allow you to mix written ideas with doodles and art and collage to fully express yourself.

Next, collect your ink pens. No pencils! Commit to your thoughts! I personally find a great deal of meaning in color, and so I keep an arsenal of green and pink and purple and red pens on me at all times.

Keep a folder or a pocket in your grimoire. This is where you can store "ingredients" for your spells: pictures, ticket stubs, a four-leaf clover, quotes, stamps, and anything else you may want to tack onto the pages of your grimoire as you curate and collect.

Dedicate the last twelve pages to a personal calendar. This is your place for remembering birthdays and death days, holidays, solstices, anniversaries, feast days, and personal annual celebrations. Every year, Jeffrey and I celebrate May 8 as Timmy Nolan Day, named after the Irish pub where we met. Create your own private holidays and invent a lasting tradition to pass down.

And then flip to the first page and trace your hand. Write your name in the middle of that. Own your grimoire with your body and mind, both of which are divine.

The secret to magic is that *you're already making it!*

Your grimoire is the tool that forces you to recognize it, record it, and remember it in times of need.

Now, what to fill it with?

If you were making a quilt, you'd gather up scraps of various materials to piece them together in a way that was beautiful to you. With a grimoire, you're doing the exact same thing. So where can you pull your materials from? Curate a library for inspiration, spells, knowledge, and fun.

I cannot begin to tell you how many times I have been asked, "What books do I start with?" These are some of the texts where I have gotten lost in wild ideas, discovered ancient practices, and amused myself with the mysteries of the universe. Your collection can be made up of memoir, fiction, history, philosophy, poetry, or anything else that sets your imagination on fire. I keep my favorites all lined up on a shelf next to my desk, separate from the other books in the house.

1. *The Long Lost Friend: A 19th Century American Grimoire* by John George Hohman

   Around the time my son was born in 2010, I was on a quest to learn more about the traditions of the Appalachian side of my family. I kept hearing about this two-hundred-year-old book. Filled with remedies and spells in the tradition of the Pennsylvania Dutch and powwow healers, it fortunately has been preserved and turned into an easily accessible paperback.

2. *Italian Folk Magic: Rue's Kitchen Witchery* by Mary-Grace Fahrun

   When my daughter was born, this was the book I curled up with, wishing for my own strong cultural heritage. We all know the Italians are magical—you've eaten their food! This book is a heartwarming and approachable collection of Italian folk magic filled with ritual blessings, magical prayers, divination techniques, crafting, and all manner of spells for things like revenge, removal, and even a spell for mothers-in-law.

3. *Witches, Midwives and Nurses* by Barbara Ehrenreich and Deirdre English
Ever notice the connection between women that were targeted as witches and their impressive skill sets? This is a revelatory portrait of how female healers have been undermined and demonized by the patriarchy because of how their power and knowledge threatened the male-dominated origins of the medical-industrial complex.

4. *The Powwow Grimoire* by Robert Phoenix
Probably my favorite book in my collection. This is a beautifully curated encyclopedia of magic from the powwow tradition of the Pennsylvania German Christian community, with instructions on how to make talismans, defend against hexes, and perform hands-on healing spells.

5. *Blackthorn's Botanical Magic: The Green Witch's Guide to Essential Oils for Spellcraft, Ritual & Healing* by Amy Blackthorn
I believe strongly that scent is the sense that creates the most powerful memories, and so I value this comprehensive handbook for magic performed with scent and essential oils.

Amy also created a line of teas that are perfect gifts for your favorite witch.

6. *Blotto Botany: A Lesson in Healing Cordials and Plant Magic* by Spencre L. R. McGowan

   This pretty little handbook caught my eye on my first trip to Salem, Massachusetts, as I perused one of my favorite shops—HausWitch. It is full of plant magic, with medicinal cordial recipes *handwritten* by the herbalist who created them. A solid starter for your potion making.

7. *Your Face Never Lies: What Your Face Reveals About You and Your Health, an Introduction to Oriental Diagnosis* by Michio Kushi

   Hear me out. I was given this petite book by my makeup artist, Wendy Bell, on *One Tree Hill*. On the surface, it just looks to be an Eastern medicine guide to understanding what the face reveals about our health and well-being. But once I realized I could diagnose a whole myriad of problems, just by looking at someone's face and eyes? Holy smokes! That skill looks like total witchcraft to the untrained observer.

8. *The Woman with the Alabaster Jar: Mary Magdalen and the Holy Grail* by Margaret Starbird

   Ms. Starbird is a firestarter! A Roman Catholic scholar who believes she found evidence that Mary Magdalene was married to Jesus Christ and gave birth to his child, she redefines "the holy grail." This book is a fascinating read and a reminder of the forgotten divine feminine.

9. *Aradia, or the Gospel of Witches: The Founding Book of Modern Witchcraft, Containing History, Traditions, Dianic Goddesses and Folklore of the Wicca* by Charles Godfrey Leland

   Sometimes known as *The Gospel of the Witches*, this book lays out the bedrock of modern witchcraft and the history and folklore of Wicca. It is the worship of Diana, her daughter Aradia, the moon, and a call to feminine power to resist the tyranny of rich and powerful men.

10. *Mary Magdalene Revealed: The First Apostle, Her Feminist Gospel & the Christianity We Haven't Tried Yet* by Meggan Watterson

   Meggan Watterson flipped everything I knew about Christianity on its head. Her close study of Mary's gospel, which was ordered to be destroyed in the fourth century but was saved by some rebellious monks, reveals a story of radical love and compassion.

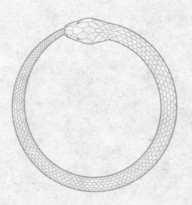

NAME YOUR HOME

ischief Farm is my home. I am loud and proud about that. My husband, Jeffrey, and I have used that name as a cornerstone for the life we've built together. Our production company is Mischief Farm Productions. The liquor brand we started together is MF Libations. At our wedding reception, we both got "Mischief" tattoos. Hell, I wrote a whole book about our journey to the farm. *The Rural Diaries* was my love letter to this magical patch of land and the people who populate it.

Mischief was the perfect word to describe the goals that Jeffrey and I had as a couple. But for those of you who haven't read *The Rural Diaries*, the name actually comes from a series of hand-carved headstones we found our first day on the property. Nestled under a gnarly old pine tree, they captured my attention immediately. Our agent told us that the solitary farmer who had owned the place for decades had an affinity for cats, and the headstones for Mischief and Mischief II were evidence of that. We left that day knowing that come hell or high water, Mischief Farm was gonna be ours.

Naming something is how we all show affection. It's why we give lovers and good friends nicknames—an inside joke that reveals intimacy and deep understanding. The world may know me as Hilarie, but the ones who call me HillBill, HillyBilly, Hillabutt, Hils . . . those are my chosen people. So, why don't we practice that same connectivity with our homes? They are deserving of affection.

Think of the thing you love most in your home. Is it your pet? I've seen signs declaring a house Casa Corgi, an homage to a four-legged family member. Maybe it's a wild creature that frequents your yard. Raven's Rest is a good name for all you *One Tree Hill* fans out there.

My husband and I once had our hearts set on a house that we'd fallen in love with at the edge of the mountains in La Quinta, California. Coyote Crossing was a labyrinth of cool, dark, terra-cotta-tiled rooms, nestled in the shadow of those haunted desert mountains. We didn't end up buying that house, but here we are, over ten years later, still waxing poetic about it. That probably would not be the case if we just called it 5**** Avenida Montezuma. Coyote Crossing has a far more mysterious appeal.

The tiny log cabin we moved into when we first fell in love with the Hudson Valley had a wide, welcoming front porch, with floorboards that bellowed deep under the weight of boots and firewood. A sign hung from a crossbeam: "The Ramble Inn." It indeed was the kind of earthy hangout where one could just ramble up and rest, casual and content.

Maybe you like a feature of your home, such as the color or the roofline. There is a feminist icon who lives not too far away, Barbara Tober. I have such a crush on her. She's been lovingly referred to as the "Jewel of Manhattan," was the editor in chief of *Brides* magazine for thirty years. Her impeccable taste created Yellowframe Farm, with sunny yellow barns dotting the pastoral rolling hills of the Hudson Valley.

On the other end of the spectrum, the steep black peaks of the House of Seven Gables—a favorite of mine—commands a great deal of respect from witches and non-witches alike in Salem, Massachusetts.

Some homes just have a one-word name. My favorite poet, Edna St. Vincent Millay, named her estate Steepletop. Elvis had Graceland. Presidents have a whole slew of instantly recognizable homes. Mount Vernon. Monticello. FDR's Springwood is right down the road from my home.

Or you can go super literal. The haunted house I lived in during my twenties? We just called her Hester's House for the ghost that was our unexpected roommate. More on her later.

We cherish the names of properties in books. It's what spans the chasm between sterile real estate and a legendary space. So, don't be timid about it! Think how different Green Gables or Hogwarts or Wuthering Heights would be if they were called by their antiseptic house number and postal code. We can do better than that!

What will you name your home? Endow it with character so that everyone from the mailman to your visiting in-laws knows what your home is about—that's where the magic lies.

We Are Water

TO MAKE A WAND FOR SEARCHING FOR WATER. On the first night of Christmas, between 11 and 12 o'clock, break off from any tree a young twig of one year's growth, in the three highest names (Father, Son and Holy Ghost), at the same time facing toward sunrise. Whenever you apply this wand in searching for anything, apply it three times. The twig must be forked, and each end of the fork must be held in one hand, so that the third and thickest part of it stands up, but do not hold it too tight. Strike the ground with the thickest end, and that which you desire will appear immediately, if there is any in the ground where you strike. The words to be spoken when the wand is thus applied are as follows:

Archangel Gabriel, I conjure thee in the name of God, the Almighty, to tell me, is there any water here or not? do tell me!

—*The Long Lost Friend: A 19th Century American Grimoire,*
by John George Hohman

*P*erhaps you've heard me talk about this before. I share this theory all the time. But I truly believe you can understand so much about a person by what body of water that person is most drawn to.

Take into consideration all the different bodies of water out there. Obviously, there are oceans. There are lakes. There are rivers and lagoons. There are bays and bayous. And the more detailed you get, the longer that list becomes.

I don't think it was a surprise to anyone when I eventually landed in a haunted house right off the banks of the Cape Fear River in North Carolina. I am an unabashed "river person."

Growing up, we lived very near the Potomac River, which acts as a boundary for much of Washington, DC; Maryland; and Northern Virginia. The Potomac is large in both size and historical importance. Right on the Potomac is Great Falls, a series of crashing waterfalls that the more adventurous would raft on the weekends while the rest of us would use it as a scenic overlook, to hike to and to make out if you were a romantic teenager.

But it was a quieter bend in that river that I connected to the most: Algonkian Regional Park. We started going to Algonkian Park when I was very little. I remember church picnics. There were games of badminton and ham sandwiches on Hawaiian sweet rolls. I remember dense trees and mulched trails through the woods. The pavilions where the mothers would gather in the shade, hollering at us to not hit each other with sticks. We had our Little League baseball team parties there. Sweet Sixteen birthday parties as we got older. And always in the background of these memories is the Potomac River.

We'd go trepidatiously as little kids, peeking at the water's edge to see tadpoles or watch the tiny fish surface. When we got older, there was a boldness to putting your feet in that river. Local legends swirled about people being swept away. There were little islands that would crop up in the middle of the rushing waters. The area was wild and unmanicured and had a Huckleberry Finn quality to it that made me feel like a character in a book, and not some ordinary kid living in the suburbs. Those wild places are so important. And I hold Algonkian and the banks of the Potomac deep in my heart.

So, now that you have a picture, think about what a river really means. It is water that is always moving. It is never, ever the same. And I suppose that's what I love so much about it. There is an ephemeral beauty that you must appreciate in the moment, because it will never return in the same way. There's unseen depth to it, an undertow that you can't necessarily understand.

A river's mystery in motion feels natural to me. I have maneuvered my entire life, always moving forward. There have been rapids at times, tumultuous falls around some of the bends. But when you hit that placid glimmering bend on an October day, there is nothing else in the world like it.

I have a lot of "ocean people" in my life, my husband being one of them. When we first met, he listened to a sound machine play ocean noises to help him sleep. The crashing of the waves soothed him in the waterless desert of New Mexico where we were staying.

My husband is someone who works tirelessly, and the ocean is a lullaby to him. He's a different person by the ocean:

it hypnotizes him into a relaxed, dreamy character. He smiles wide when the salt air hits him, and it's fun to watch him unfurl and just be when he's stoking a beach bonfire at night with the moon reflecting on the waves. It doesn't matter which ocean. We've been to Massachusetts and Virginia and Miami and Los Angeles and Hawaii and Barcelona and New Zealand, and the result is always the same. The lapping of those waves makes him feel safe. Ocean people find comfort in going and returning and going and returning repeatedly, like the waves on the sand. That's exactly how my Jeffrey exists, darting off to distant places for work, always to return to us here at Mischief Farm. I love that idea, that there are people who can find beauty in the return. As a river person focused on looking forward, I marvel at that ability, and on the occasions when I get homesick, I wish I were more like that.

Then there are my lake friends. Calm and placid on the surface, with deep, dark, unknown depths. You can see their clearly defined boundaries and the fun they bring, what with water skis and tubes and such. But what lurks in those depths? Do they harbor a Loch Ness creature in their life? Are there pockets of icy water?

I love the mystery of my bayou friends. If you've never taken an airboat tour through a swamp, do it at least once in your life. The waterways are covered with tiny floating plants, so you don't feel like you're in water, but rather gliding on an avenue of fluorescent green lawn. Spanish moss hanging off the cypress trees obscures what's around the bend. And perhaps that's what I love most about bayou people: their ability to keep moving forward even when they don't know what's coming. There's a myriad of things that can kill you in the swamp; it's a risky place to hang out. But I've always been partial to gamblers.

We may as well address pool people while we're here. There's not a damn thing wrong with pool people. They like things tidy. Clear. Sanitized. They want to be able to see the bottom, to heat the water, to be in control. It's good to have a couple of those folks in your world, and it's perfectly fine to admit you're one of them! They are the best party planners and great collaborators. Not all of us can be wild sea creatures!

What are you? Your body is made of at least 55 percent water.

Stop and really think about which bodies of water excite the H_2O in you. Maybe your 55 percent was mostly ocean at one point. Perhaps your water ran as a creek cutting through a mountain once upon a time. The liquid in your body might have kept the secrets of a deep, dark lake. I don't think it's outlandish to say we carry that energy around with us. So, identify what your safe water is and surround yourself with that imagery and energy. Keep seashells on your windowsill or river rocks at your desk. Keep an ancient cypress knee on the back deck. Or ya know . . . go swim in your pool. Whatever floats your boat. Literally.

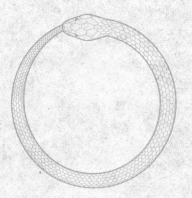

ITHACA

 've called several places home over the years: Hester's House, The Ramble Inn, Mischief Farm. Each with a name as unique and special as the houses themselves. But my home—my real home, the place that made me, the nest in my heart—is Ithaca.

For those of you who don't remember Greek mythology from middle school English class, lemme give you the rundown on Ithaca, immortalized in Homer's *The Odyssey*.

An island dotting the Ionian Sea in Greece, Ithaca is the home of King Odysseus and his wife, Penelope. The Trojan War breaks out and Odysseus pretends to be insane so that he doesn't have to leave the home he loves to go fight. The dude is found out and has to join the Greek army, where he is responsible for the infamous Trojan Horse idea. This war lasts a full decade! And when it's finally over, Odysseus can't wait to get home to his wife and his beloved Ithaca.

But—there is always a but in mythology—he makes a misstep and ends up blinding Poseidon's son, a Cyclops. This enrages the sea god, who takes revenge by thwarting Odysseus's journey for another ten years. During that time, he faces giant cannibals; the enchantress Circe, who turns his crew into pigs and makes him her captive lover; the Sirens, who threaten to destroy anyone who tries to pass them; a couple of sea monsters; and the nymph Calypso, who also captured him as a lover (rough life, Odysseus). All the while yearning to return to the home of his heart.

Odysseus finally makes it home after twenty years, only to find all these other guys trying to marry Penelope. He pretty much kills them all, reclaims his throne as the King of Ithaca, and all seems well. But I can't help but wonder if it really was a happy ending.

The Ithaca of his mind, the home he yearned and fought for— is that really what he returned to? Twenty years had passed. Can we ever truly return home?

WE SOLD MY OWN CHILDHOOD HOME IN 1998, THE SUMMER before my junior year in high school. 105 North Ithaca Road. Yes, *Ithaca*.

My family moved across town to an endless labyrinth of cul-de-sacs and unsold lots, newly laid white concrete curbs bled over by the fields of red Virginia clay. This subdivision had been the circus grounds; I'd seen an elephant paraded around with kids on its back just a few short years before.

I never quite felt at home there; I always referred to that new place as "my parents' house." My house—my Ithaca—was that old two-story center-hall colonial nestled in a 1960s-era suburb where most of the streets are named after presidents. It was the house with marigold-yellow appliances and a plastic shopping bag full of other plastic shopping bags hanging from the knob of the pantry door. Ours was the house with two metal swing sets in the back, dusty patches of bare earth beneath the gliders and swings. My home had a mudroom off the carport, where I'd hide out next to the washing machine while extending the curly phone cord as far as I possibly could under the louvered door.

It had carpeted stairs and a formal dining room we weren't allowed to enter and a bright red front door. The exterior had been baby blue with burgundy shutters in the mid-eighties when we first moved in and hung a swinging bench under the massive oak in the backyard. Ten years later, a storm would rip half the vinyl siding off and an insurance payout would allow my parents to upgrade to a sunny yellow exterior, with Charleston-green shutters. The red door remained.

Then there was my room.

It sat at the front corner of the house, surrounded by massive, feathery pine trees. They gave the room a dreamy quality, a coolness in the thick heat of Virginia summers, and a Christmas card coziness during the sharp winter months. The trees were confidants that I'd act out my wildest ambitions with, singing "Somewhere Out There" from *An American Tail* while pretending to be on *Star Search* as their boughs applauded. They helped me plan escape routes after watching hours of *Unsolved Mysteries* and *America's Most Wanted*, figuring it was only a matter of time before intruders would force me to leap into the arms of my tree friends and shimmy down to safety. My twin mattress was my treehouse bed, surrounded by green filtered light and the sound of long needles sweeping against the window screens. I'd lie there, floating in that cacophony of clutter and childhood collections.

I wrote the names of my enemies inside the deepest corner of my closet with the worst cusses I knew. I dropped acrylic paint all over the carpet while in the midst of elaborate craft projects and became skilled at taking nail scissors to trim it out once it had dried, subtly altering the topography of the room. My nightstand held two wide-set drawers of cassette tapes, with my boom box in the shape of a '57 Chevy sitting atop. A photocopy of an auto-graphed Ray Bradbury headshot was taped up above that.

There was a tall bookshelf in the corner—cast-off office furniture—with a fold-down desk that seemed perfectly suited to hide the various journals I started, kept, started again, and then buried. Shelves of books I meant to read again and dolls that I was sure came to life at night. Trinkets and flowers plucked from outside and dried—or worse, molded into place—in the various junk and jewelry and treasure boxes I accumulated. There was another desk littered at times with a sewing machine and scraps of clothes that I'd grown out of but had planned to Maria von Trapp into garments for Barbies, or a chunky typewriter with a fickle ribbon that would make me feel like Lois Lane when it decided to work.

The vent in the floor of my room connected to the vent in my brothers' room down the hall. We'd pull off the grates on summer nights and whisper to each other while frigid metallic air numbed our noses.

Like Odysseus, I yearn for that house; I would give anything to return to that room. To take my kids there. To lie in bed with my daughter and read *The Doll in the Garden* or *Afternoon of the Elves*. Or to spread out on the floor with my son and pull the old shoe boxes full of craft supplies from under my bed, laugh with him at the unfinished projects tucked back into those boxes, and marvel at the potential his childhood creativity would see in the collections of trash.

We can't go back. And while my heart hurts to be unable to share that with them, I carry those memories with me to the floor of the rooms we've created together in our home, where we play make-believe and read books and glue together messy crafts made of bits and bobs, odds and ends. I may yearn for my Ithaca, but every day I am creating Ithaca for my children here.

I did return to my Ithaca after my daughter was born. It was as if an internal compass kept pointing me home. Like Odysseus, I'd spent twenty years battling repulsive monsters (*cough* our bosses on One Tree Hill *cough*), doomed love affairs, work that took me to cities in which I didn't belong, and exciting—albeit exhausting—adventures.

It was time to go back to the home of my heart.

Altars

If I could start again, I would install an altar within me.
I would place the most sacred object inside it: my own
heart.

—Meggan Watterson, *Mary Magdalene Revealed*

*W*hat spaces are sacred to you?

My childhood bedroom—particularly the fold-down
desk—was indeed my first altar.

Can you remember yours? Was it on your nightstand or
in your bathroom? Or your tree house? Did you keep a little
corner of your school desk or your locker as a place to display
your trinkets and treasures?

It is at this point that I urge you to open up your grimoire
and make a list of every minute detail you can remember about
the home of your heart. It could be your childhood bedroom. Or
your first apartment, or that magical bunk from summer camp
the year you came into your own. Write it all down. Make a map

with your words. Then you'll have the tools to re-create your safe space one day when you need it most.

My fold-down desk worked as an altar for me because I could easily close it up. *Nothing to see here, folks!*

I kept my *Secret Garden*-themed diary there. I also had a lace bear filled with rose petals and potpourri that my dad had brought home from a work trip. I had a piggy bank made out of Delftware, a gift from my Dutch relatives. It played the song "Edelweiss" from *The Sound of Music*, the very first play I was ever in. In the springtime, I had a habit of picking the buds off the big maple tree in our backyard. That deep red color is something I've always wanted to capture and never quite could, and I kept the buds in a little silver bowl. That practice is my first memory of feeling witchy.

When I got a bit older and started middle school, there were a couple of mystical shops in our area. One was in the nondescript 1970s shopping center close to our house, right smack dab between the dentist and some real estate offices. It was upstairs, and it felt taboo to climb up there and sift through the incense and crystals, almost as if it had been purposely placed where you couldn't be seen shopping for your pagan practices. Ooooohhh, I felt positively wicked!

The other shop, however, was on the main street in Leesburg—the historic town center. It was right out there in the open with huge plate-glass windows. It was downright audacious to be announcing yourself in the community as the kind of person who would go shopping in that establishment. My nerdy little wannabe witch heart loved the incense, and so I'd buy bundles of it in long, fragile sticks and keep them on my pull-down altar.

I grew up in the church, so I knew altars to be sacred spaces. In the Evangelical Lutheran church of my early childhood, it was a pretty big responsibility to be the person who provided floral arrangements for the Sunday service. I remember feeling pangs of jealousy that the boys in the church were permitted to help gather the offering and take it to the flower-festooned tables up front. No girls allowed. We switched over to the Methodist church when I was in middle school, and it had a very different vibe. Everyone was welcome up at that altar, whether for communion or the children's story-time part of the service. We did hokey little plays up there, as well as bell choir. I even used to go on dates to church once I was in high school. Still, the altar remained a sacred space. I never really considered that I was using space in my own home in much the same way.

Take a look around the homes of your loved ones. Does Grandma have a side table in her living room where her most beloved photos and tchotchkes are displayed? Does your uncle have a shelf of signed baseballs or framed tickets from that legendary game he talks about every Thanksgiving?

It's important to pay attention to how we devote space.

So, identify a location in your home that you come into contact with on a daily basis.

You know that little rhyme people recite at weddings? *Something old, something new, something borrowed, something blue*. There's something to that!

Populate your altar with items that are old, to remind you of who you were. (Childhood toys. Old photographs. Ancestors' jewelry.)

Sprinkle it with items that are new to commit to who you are now. (Trinkets from recent adventures. Found pennies. Written-down intentions.)

Ground yourself with earth energy. (Dried flowers. Crystals that catch your eye. Acorns.)

Protect yourself with talismans. (Saint medallions. Prayer beads. Sator squares.)

Add items to inspire you. To delight you. Make it a space in your home where you can center yourself and feel known.

My current altar is right next to my kitchen sink. Each night as I wash dishes, I run through the items there in my head. A glass butterfly from my goddaughter as a thank you for believing in fairies. Dried flowers from my husband. Rue cuttings in a jar from my witch sister Mary-Grace Fahrun. A pendant of the Three Graces. A pottery skull box that Gus painted as a wee one. A deer jaw we found in the woods. A candle bought in Salem, just waiting for the right spell. It's a space that makes my mundane housework feel like an opportunity to reflect.

Give yourself that space. Access to the divine and sacred isn't limited to religious establishments or the elite. It is your birthright. An altar that is a part of your everyday routine becomes a place to whisper gratitudes, utter protections over loved ones, or remember people and places and times. These are the practices that transform chores into magical rituals, conjuring your creativity.

FOUNTAIN OF YOUTH

n September 2018, with a baby on my hip and my son at my side, I went back into my high school for the first time in almost two decades. In the front entryway, there was the school crest, something I helped design during my senior year.

Within the walls of Park View High School, I had fallen in love with acting as Gretl in *The Sound of Music*. I had experimented heavily with my identity, sometimes becoming a preppy cheerleader and sometimes an androgynous emo girl. I'd been the kid that joined damn near every extracurricular activity in school, from Forensics to German club. And I had been taken in by two of my greatest mentors in life: Bruce and Bobbie Johnson. Mr. Johnson was the Latin teacher and Bobbie, his wife, was my government teacher. And together they served as our student government sponsors. Being in those hallways—the love, the learning, the fun—it all came back to me.

I stood in the main office while they did morning announcements, and soon enough it was time for the pep rally.

It was like *time travel*.

When I was a student there, Park View High School's pep rallies were legendary. In the late 1990s, my school was a football empire. Friday mornings in the fall buzzed with a vibrant youthful energy, enhanced by the fact that our team was good. Like really, *really* good. From my eighth-grade year cheering for the rec league Rams until my senior year, our boys lost only two games. Banners were painted. Senior Court was decorated. Letter jackets abounded. It was a sea of red, white, and blue to cheer on the unstoppable Patriots.

But the pep rallies, you guys . . . the PEP RALLIES!! Movies and television series *wish* they could create the all-American fervor of a Park View pep rally. Teenagers have a bad rap for being jaded or "too cool for school." And that's an assumption that was floating around well before iPhones and social media took over the younger generations' brains. When I was a kid, it was hip-hop and video games that allegedly made us cold-hearted misanthropes. I digress.

It didn't matter if you were a jock or a goth or a science fair genius or a strange combination of high school stereotypes. The entire student body would funnel into the gym mid-morning with the thunderous sound of twelve hundred bodies climbing into the wooden stands. Freshmen, sophomores, juniors, and seniors all took their respective corners, competitive in their quest to out-shout each other. My senior year, it was my greatest adolescent achievement to combine my two deep loves—drama and cheerleading—by employing the Theater Department to bring in smoke machines and wild lighting and large props left over from productions to celebrate the football team's path to glory. It built a bridge—two painfully different groups of kids uniting over a common goal: kicking our rival's ass.

Is it all kind of silly in hindsight? Sure. Is it solving world hunger or fixing poverty?

No . . . or is it?

See, what happened during those Fridays way back when is that we all formed an alliance. As school let out, the principal played our rallying song, Whitesnake's "Here I Go Again," over the loudspeaker, and many of us lingered in the parking lot, singing along and being idiots. Only we weren't alone. We were a team.

Pregame, we'd pack the stands while the marching band banged on buckets and taunted the opposing side with horns and brass and sass. We cruised the parking lot of the Sterling Shopping Plaza after our victories, in our parade of early eighties hand-me-down cars.

I think you get it. Park View was a real-life *Friday Night Lights, Varsity Blues, Remember the Titans*. Football was king, but it was also inclusive. The whole damn school liked winning.

Color me surprised when less than twenty years later, the unthinkable happened.

A flare had gone up among the Facebook friends from Sterling I'd remained in touch with. My inbox was flooded. *Did you see this? Oh my God! How could this happen??*

No, friends, there was not a natural disaster or violent tragedy.

Our Park View student body was safe. But another misfortune had
fallen upon our alma mater: Park View High School had lost its
varsity football team.

What the absolute fuck??

I REACHED OUT TO A FEW PEOPLE I COULD TRUST TO TELL ME
what was really going on. The Johnsons had opened the school
in the 1970s—they had known my mother when she was in the
first graduating class of Park View. I knew they would level with
me. They truly loved that community and wanted the best for it
and for the kids at Park View. They always had. Bruce told me
about the politics of it all—the demographics, the money, and the
racism. The more they told me, the more curious I got.

After doing some research, I learned that my alma mater, Park
View High School, had become a Title One school in the years
that I'd been away. Honestly, I was unsure of the specifics of what
that meant when I first heard it. But it means that roughly half
the student body qualifies for low-income assistance. Back when
I was a student, the high school was mostly made up of kids who
came from middle-class families. Over the years, the demographics of the area shifted, and as housing developments and brand-
spankin'-new shopping centers and McMansions went up, the
old communities were left in the dust. Park View is hands down
the most diverse of all these communities, with a school popu-
lation that is, according to *U.S. News & World Report*, 89 percent
minority. No other school in the county even comes close. The
walls of the dated building are filled with asbestos. The ceilings
are water stained and falling down. The bathrooms work . . .
occasionally. Simultaneously, the county Park View is situated

in, Loudoun County, was listed among the top five wealthiest counties in the nation by *Forbes* magazine multiple years in a row.

Something wasn't adding up.

I started making calls—first to the athletic director. He filled me in on the practicalities of high school sports—the cost of medical insurance, the cleats, the equipment, the camps. How the commitment to participate in an after-school sport means that you need transportation. It means that you can't take an after-school job. It means that you can't commit to work on the weekends, either. I'd never really thought of participating in high school sports as a luxury. It was more something you did so that your college applications would look well rounded. But I have no idea how students whose families depend on their financial participation would juggle that schedule. And to add classwork on top of all that is impossible. (Listen, I worry about brain injuries as a result of playing football just as much as the next mother. But I also don't want any kid to not have an opportunity based on resources.)

After speaking with the athletic director, I got connected with the principal. Turns out it wasn't just football that was suffering at Park View. It wasn't even just the sports. *All* of the extracurricular programs were lagging.

I learned about school budgets and about Loudoun County's "equality over equity" plans, which meant they gave every single school in the county the exact same amount of support. Sounds good on paper, right? But what it really meant was that the kids who attended schools in more affluent areas could supplement their budgets with ticket sales from sporting events, where they had robust attendance. They had fundraisers where parents could solicit their wealthy coworkers to donate and get involved.

I learned about theater programs at neighboring high schools that raised scholarship funds in the *millions*. But for a school like Park View, their chunk of money had to stretch in a very different way. Their budget went to feeding many of these kids three times a day.

They had to create an on-site food and toiletry pantry so that kids in need could take essentials home. They had students using the washing machines at the school or coming into the building at 5 a.m. after working all-night shifts stocking grocery shelves to sleep on the beds in the nurse's office. That little chunk of money didn't get to go toward field trips, nicer facilities, or equipment, and there certainly wasn't enough for after-school programs. The school was taking on far more than educational responsibilities. And I wouldn't have known any of this if it hadn't been for that damn football team!

I'd been fighting to find my way back home, when all along, my home was needing me to fight for it.

I wanted to help, and was determined to set up a nonprofit board that would give financial support to all extracurriculars for the students. I knew I couldn't do it alone, so I started making calls to other Park View alums. First, I called my best friend, Ashley Dawson Hoyt. We've been attached at the hip since sixth grade, when we both started doing plays after school. Literally, the very first conversation we ever had was standing by the lockers, comparing how many lines we'd each been given in the fall production. Needless to say, we were ambitious. We were both student government kids and Ashley, being the nicest girl in our entire grade, was naturally class president. Thank my lucky stars, today she is a kick-ass accountant. I don't know if she ever felt like she had a choice, but God bless her, when I asked if she would be the treasurer if I set up a nonprofit board, she showed up. She's a golden human.

As for the legal help of setting up an LLC and getting nonprofit status, Kathleen Oare DiSanto was the first person who came to mind. A few years younger than us, I knew that she was incredibly bright, and she had been the only girl on the football team. That's right, friends. This teeny tiny girl decided to go out for the football team. And watching her in uniform made all of us—even us older girls—incredibly proud. She's now a mother of many, and a powerful lawyer.

What I really needed was someone in the community still tied to sports. Of the Park View supporters commenting on Facebook about how these kids deserved better, one voice became increasingly louder: Tony Canonico.

Let me just paint a lil' picture. It's 1998, a school dance after a basketball game.

There's a sick slow jam playing—probably some Boyz II Men or K-Ci & JoJo. From across the room one of the cool seniors, in his puka shell necklace and Abercrombie sweater, parts the crowd and asks you to dance. Oh. My. God. Tony Canonico was the "Italian Stallion" of Park View High School. Or at least that's what we underclassmen girls called him. Tony was the kind of football player who was still nice to the other groups of kids. He was cool without being condescending. And he came from a family that got involved in the community. As luck would have it, these days he was also working with a local sports organization that provided high-end camps and facilities for the ever-growing youth sports world in Northern Virginia. Tony spoke the language and knew all the players that we would need to get on our side to save sports at Park View.

We had conference calls. We filed paperwork. We lobbied hard on behalf of these kids. And Project Patriot was born in August of 2018.

I asked the principal if it would be all right if I stopped by the school when I was in the area next month.

"Well, there's gonna be a pep rally," he told me. "Would you be okay speaking at that?"

A PEP RALLY?

I don't think this man understood how excited I was. But in my mind, there was no way the current student body would be as dorky as we were when we were kids. Kids now are different, right?

And so, in September, my children stood on the basketball court as those twelve hundred kids painted a picture of all the boring mom-stories I'd told Gus on the drive up.

My son was enthralled. George bounced in Bobbie Johnson's arms.

Each grade came in wearing their assigned colors so that you could tell freshmen from sophomores and juniors from seniors. They packed those wooden bleachers, the very same ones that I'd climbed as a fourteen-year-old. The stomping and the clapping and the cheering and the wild participation . . . hanging back against the wall with my own friends and former teachers, we realized, *the magic was still real.*

The love in that building was still real. It was explosive and exciting and inspiring.

The thundering of each grade, vying for the coveted spirit stick, echoed exactly the same as it did in my memory.

These kids didn't even have a varsity football team to cheer for, and yet they were on their feet, exuberant in their sense of belonging. This was their school. It was their turf. It didn't matter what anyone said about them.

At the end, the junior class was awarded a spirit stick. It was just a simple wooden dowel painted and covered with glitter. But you could tell it meant as much to them as it did to us twenty years before.

And so, when I spoke to those kids, I told them that whatever they thought they would be getting out of Project Patriot, I promised I was getting so much more.

I got to return to Ithaca. Something I thought didn't exist anymore.

My childhood home had been sold. My neighbors and relatives had all moved away.

And yet here was this glimmering piece of my childhood, perfectly preserved.

After it was over, I loaded Gus and George up into my car, parked in the same lot I used to hang out in every day as a seventeen-year-old.

I didn't know what to do. I couldn't go back to the hotel. I had just gone back to my Ithaca. My heart would have wept to break that spell.

I put the car in gear and found myself driving toward my middle school. I sat there telling my son stories that he suddenly had a much more invested interest in.

I drove to the elementary school building, Gus marveling that it looked so much like his own school.

I showed my children the water tower where my father had convinced us a monster lived.

And then, after turning down East Holly Avenue, I took a left onto my own road. My house stood on the left.

It was different. But the same. I parked awkwardly, just trying to take it all in.

There had been a massive lilac bush when I was little. Actually, it was a cluster of lilacs fused together. It was a springtime wonder, offering a scent like no other. (How come as a kid, lilac seasons seem to last so long? I remember endless days in her fragrant arms. Now as an adult, the moment they bloom, my clock tracks less than a week of perfection. Time moves differently.) Concrete for a swimming pool and basketball court had killed the lilacs. But the Japanese maple remained right outside the big bay window. We used to hide in there, treating it like an open umbrella. The ground beneath it was soft from the accumulation of fallen leaves. Loamy. The light inside tinted red.

The maple tree by the road also remained. I'd hid in its branches so many days, reading books, spying on kids who were allowed to leave their yards. I'd been Harriet the Spy up there, with my marble-covered composition notebook, writing missives no one was ever supposed to see in my baby grimoire. But the massive pine trees that had shadowed my childhood bedroom were gone. Not even stumps remained. The front corner of the house stood there glaring in the afternoon sun. I felt embarrassed, like seeing someone you love naked in public.

A car pulled into the driveway across the street. A teen boy got out of the passenger seat. He glanced over, and then did a double take.

"Hi." I waved, trying to seem casual.

"Hi. Were you the lady at my school today?"

Fuck. *Lady??* I had been a sprite on this street, an urchin, a princess, a little witch. Now I was an old lady.

"Yep," I answered. "You have fun at the pep rally?"

"Yeah!" he responded, genuinely enthused. "We won the spirit stick."

"You're a junior."

"Yes, ma'am." There was an awkward pause. "Do you know the person who lives there?"

He motioned toward my house.

"I don't," I admitted. "I grew up in this house."

"What?" He was incredulous. My introduction at the high school that day had included a list of professional accomplishments and my offer to send any kid who wanted to play football to camp.

"That was my room up there," I said, pointing at the naked corner.

"I had no idea you lived there. I could introduce you to the lady who lives there now." This kid was nice. Like a boy from a movie. Helpful, handsome. It made me happy and proud. The street that had remained unchanged for twenty years was still churning out wholesome, unjaded kids.

"She's really nice. I'm sure she'd let you in. Do you want me to ask?"

I thought about it. I couldn't see the couches and TVs and tables in the wrong places. It would shatter me to see renovated bathrooms. The updated kitchen would ruin the experience. My bedroom should always have the twin bed in the corner, a desk with a sewing machine, a bookshelf with all my treasures out on display and the soft green glow of light filtered through feathery pines. Some things are better left how we remember them.

Gus and George started fidgeting in the backseat. "I gotta get these kids fed. But please tell her I said hi. I love this house." We rolled away, leaving North Ithaca Road.

I'd lost the physical home on Ithaca, but my experience that day in that dated gym from the 1970s with a pack of twelve hundred howling, hopeful kids . . . that was home. Connecting with my classmates and former teachers, and former classmates who are now teachers themselves . . . that was home.

✦

Years later I am proud to report that not only is football back at Park View, but all the sports have been gaining steam. I follow their social media accounts and cheer like a proud mama bear when the Lady Patriot teams bring home a victory, or our soccer team excels, or even when we lose but do it with style and grace. Because the most important part of all of this was never winning. It was showing up.

And show up we did. Over forty years of alumni have begun rallying for our old stomping grounds.

We did T-shirt sales with Represent that funded that first year of spending. "High School Forever" became our logo and call to arms. The wish lists the teachers created were posted online and were tackled by a flood of generosity from other PV graduates. My manager, Liz DeCesare, secured corporate donations and the Washington Commanders got involved. We even got Nike to come in and donate cleats for all the football players. It took a couple of years to get that program back up and running. But there we all were again, old classmates from drama and science club and sports and student government, standing up for the current students of Park View.

Just recently, one of my neighbors from the years on Ithaca became the PTSA president. Amy Gazes and I rode the bus together, and now her son is playing football and her daughter is in marching band. She has become a total queen, rallying support not only for the programming of the school, but for the teachers and the Sterling Park community as a whole.

Now, what started off as a group project to save football has turned into an all-out army of proud Patriots. Park View is one of the oldest schools in the county. These families, these kids, and this building deserve our unyielding support. So, we gather together and get to be seventeen again. We show up for those games and pep rallies. We're still singing Whitesnake's *"Here I go again on my own . . ."* Only we aren't on our own. We never were.

Park View gatherings are raucous affairs, legendary among the ever-growing sprawl of McMansions and freshly constructed high schools in the county with names that create the illusion of heritage. Riverside. Freedom. Dominion. The rich kids can keep their brand-new stadiums and equipment and professional-grade auditoriums and private coaching clinics for athletes and artists alike. They can have their parent-funded goodies that the Title One families can never keep up with. They can keep their parking lots full of Lexus and BMWs, their wealth and their overwhelming whiteness. Park View—opened during America's Bicentennial in 1976—is home of the Patriots. These are kids who work harder with fewer resources. They are kids who don't have any illusions about privilege. They are tough and wildly polite and oh my GOD, do they know how to throw a pep rally!

Talismans for Your Rebellion

The purpose of a talisman is to attract a specific influence into the bearer's life. This could be strength, protection, luck, prosperity, love, abundance, or any other influence or thing the individual wishes to attract. Talismans bring something toward you.

—Robert Phoenix, *The Powwow Grimoire*

*W*anna feel young again? Want to experience that rush of rebellion and community that made you feel alive when you were seventeen? Has the same-old, same-old routine got you feeling like you're a cyborg, programmed to work, clean, eat, clean, and stare at a screen?

Revolt! I mean it. Find a cause for good and fight like hell for it.

Magic has always been about rebellion.

What's your passion? Animals? Find that shelter that needs a warrior. Kids? I was fortunate enough to find Astor Services here in Rhinebeck, New York, at a time in my life when I needed something in which to pour some love. As a result of getting involved there, we renovated the entire residential wing *and* I made some of the most important friendships of my life.

You have a heart for veterans? Wounded Warrior Project is amazing. Habitat for Humanity is always a rewarding place to get your hands dirty. Are you like me and furious about banned books? Set up a Little Free Library in your front yard and make sure that important works and marginalized voices are easily accessible. Or find the most obscure little hole-in-the-wall organization and make it your goal to shower it with love. Collaboration and purpose keep us young and gorgeous!

If you are going to head into battle, you need to protect yourself. Talismans and jewelry can bring comfort and protection as we move through the world. You probably didn't even realize you were already engaging in this age-old practice. But every culture and religion has such objects. Some are more obvious than others. Your talisman could be a lucky rabbit's foot, your astrological sign, a stone with a particular significance, or a piece of nature from a place that's special to you. Our Christian friends adorn themselves with the Holy Cross, while our Jewish loved ones touch the mezuzah on the doorframe before they enter a home. The Seal of Solomon, also known as the Star of David, is also largely associated with the Jewish faith, but that's a fairly recent thing. Before the 1600s, this symbol had been recognized by numerous cultures for centuries as the marriage of opposites. Masculine and feminine. *As above, so below.*

Another symbol that has spanned the globe is the evil eye, used to turn away hexes and negativity and ill intentions. From Turkey to Greece, Portugal to Iran, it's an instantly recognizable symbol that dates back to 3300 BC. My friend Sharagim has one on at all times. Well, maybe more than one. They dangle from her ears and adorn her wrist, while a twinkly gemstone evil eye guards her collarbone on a gold chain. She is generous with them, placing red threads with the symbol on them on my own wrist, never breaking eye contact. She has placed glass evil-eye pebbles in my pockets and given me key chains to see me home safely. "If they break? You don't touch them," she has warned me. "It means there was a curse that has been avoided. The eye worked." Noted. She also gathers rings when she travels to visit family in Iran. I can't tell you how many times I've been in a high-stress situation where she's whipped an amethyst or lapis lazuli stone ring from her pocket and put it on my finger. "Wear it until this is over." Somehow, the rings always fit, and her brand of talisman magic has seen me through miscarriages, professional crises, family drama, and medical emergencies.

Catholics don medals of the saints for specific protections, like a St. Christopher medal when they're traveling. I found Catholic medals hanging as protective elements in two of my homes—one in Hester's House, and the other in the grandma house on Mischief Farm. And after I prayed at the shrine of Mary Magdalene to get pregnant, only to conceive George a month later, I now give Magdalene medals to any of my girl-friends who are struggling with infertility.

Sator squares are a symbol that can seem more occult oriented than biblical. But do a little digging and you'll learn that this powerful talisman was a secret symbol that early Christians used to identify one another. The square is a palindrome, the same backwards and forward, up and down. And while it translates from Latin to a seemingly meaningless line about a farmer sowing seeds, it's an anagram that rearranges to *Pater Noster,* or "Our Father," the beginning of the Lord's Prayer. The anagram leaves two extra A's and two extra O's, symbolizing the Alpha and Omega, which is exactly how Christ referred to himself. This is a common charm seen carved into the ruins of antiquity and ramshackle cabins of Appalachia. I like to make Sator squares from clay, stamping the letters in before baking, or use a heated branding iron to burn them into wood objects. Place them in your home or car or any other place you want protection.

```
S   A   T   O   R

A   R   E   P   O

T   E   N   E   T

O   P   E   R   A

R   O   T   A   S
```

Decide what is sacred to you and write those things on stones or parchment or paper and tuck them into an amulet, plant them in your garden, display them out in the open, or hide them away as your own personal secret. A talisman can be made from anything that is meaningful to you because *you* imbue it with your intention and power. It is the physical representation of your care and good intentions for your loved ones and sacred spaces.

STORYTELLING

veryone loves an urban legend, right?

Urban legends have spawned countless books and movies and songs. I used to love those songs from the 1950s and '60s that told horrible sad stories about someone's boyfriend or girlfriend dying after a series of poor choices. "Leader of the Pack." "Last Kiss." "Tell Laura I Love Her." "Teen Angel." "Endless Sleep." Teenagers are doomed! I also came of age right at the rebirth of Teen Scream movies. Freshman year in high school, my friends and I lied to our parents and said we were going to see *Jerry Maguire*. We did not. Instead, we sneaked into *Scream* and were ruined forever. The success of that movie ensured that my high school years were filled with busty ingenues running from all kinds of urban legends—dudes with hooks, classmates with knives, lots of masks, teachers who were aliens. You get it.

These are stories that live for decades, or centuries even. And for good cause! Gatherin' around to share in our creativity is a basic human impulse. Gatherin' around to scare the hell out of each other? Helps weed out the weenies. It's a good way of finding your tribe and your particular brand of weirdness.

Growing up, my dad was the storyteller in our family. I knew that the area we lived in had only been developed in the 1960s, before which it was a huge stretch of rolling hills and pastoral farmland. The Appalachian Mountains surrounded us. And so, when my father told me the story of the farmer whose wife complained of something scratching at the door, I could visualize it perfectly. When he told me that the farmer's wife left the house at night and shortly thereafter the farmer heard a scratching at the door? I could feel the dread bubbling up. When the farmer shot through the door thinking it was a legendary panther that had been stalking the area, only to find his slain wife outside the door, I fully believed that this story had happened in the rural Virginia farmlands! I was well into adulthood before I found out that was a story that people told everywhere.

But then, other stories were specifically ours.

We lived in the shadow of the Sterling water tower, a large barrel that shot up five or six stories next to Sully Elementary School. It was bluish in color with big red stripes that ran up the sides, with a tiny service staircase that ran up the side to the top. As my friends and I walked home from school, we got an up-close look at that water tower every single day.

It was nothing particularly special, but it was a strange thing to have nestled right in the middle of our residential streets and cul-de-sacs. In elementary school, we talked real big about who was going to climb that damn staircase and spray-paint their name on the top. For so many years, that was the worst thing I could think of for a kid to do.

But then our dad told us a story about the water tower that put it into mythological space.

The local pastor's family lived next door to us, and their youngest kid was named Johnny. It was one of those long, drawn-out, hot summer days where the Virginia clay turns everything into an orange haze, and Johnny was in our yard asking my dad a question that had been pestering him.

"Mr. Burton," he said. "How'd you lose your hair on either side of your head?"

I don't think Johnny was trying to be mean, he was just curious, but still, *fucking kids*. My father had a mean widow's peak, and it wasn't anything he tried to disguise. He also had a thick black mustache that matched his dark hair and his even darker sense of humor. More than one person compared him to the Goth King, Edgar Allan Poe.

"Well, Johnny," he said. "You ever hear about the Claw?"

"The Claw? Gosh no," Johnny replied.

"Look over there." And from the chain-link confines of our backyard, my father pointed to the top of the water tower. "Up there is where the Claw is."

Okay, so I'd never heard about this or seen any evidence of something living on top of the water tower. But my father had a mystique about him. He was involved in the military, had been a Green Beret and in the reserves, and sometimes he would go away for chunks of time that weren't really explained to us. But we knew that he did training exercises and wore a uniform and was very official when need be. He went on to explain:

There'd been a series of missing children in the community, specifically girls. It's why all the parents were being real fussy about letting kids walk to school. One by one, local girls had gone missing, and the police had no idea who had taken them. There was a panic, and my father's military buddies were called up to start taking a look around. Well, his buddy Little Andy got everybody into a helicopter, and they decided to survey Sterling Park from the air.

To their horror, they saw all the girls tied up on top of the water tower with an appalling BEAST keeping watch over them. It was hairy, like Bigfoot, with a hunched back and too-long arms like a sloth. Each limb contained two revolting claws. The beast spotted them and started acting erratically. After landing the helicopter, my father and his friends formulated a plan. They would wait until the beast was asleep and go up and gather those girls in the dead of night, one by one. In the wee hours of the morning, they climbed that tiny service ladder, shushing the victims. Slowly, they tiptoed under the monster's nose until it was time to get the last girl.

Naturally, my father was the last one up there. And as the beast woke up and roared in fury, my father grabbed this girl and passed her down below to his waiting cohorts. She was safe, but he was NOT! Because as he descended the ladder, the Claw whipped down his arm and those razor-sharp talons hooked him right on the top of his head. My father lost grip of the service ladder and was dangling by his scalp. And then in true eighties fashion, my dad's buddies pulled out machine guns and slaughtered the Claw, setting my father free but also scarring him for life with those patches on either side of his head that wouldn't grow hair.

Whew.

Poor Johnny must have felt like a real jackass for bringing up something so traumatic. But I appreciate that my father took something that other men would have felt bashful about and turned it into a hero's journey. Odysseus of the backyard. Needless to say, the Claw disappeared from the community, but the possibility of a Claw being up there never left. Who knows what lingered on top of the water tower in the following years?

Even now as a grown-up, I see it as a mysterious, intimidating place. When I brought my kids back to Ithaca, I let them know that's where the Claw lived. And they didn't question it. They just accepted it as fact.

I loved growing up in a place like that, where stories could abound. We were told about the mystery of the Bunny Man in Clifton, Virginia, where my father's family lived.

This is a nationally known legend about a lunatic who dressed up like a bunny and hacked up teenagers with an ax. Journalists have dug into the truth of that story and found a little of it to be real and a lot of it to be fabrication. But I once looked at an overhead map of where my father's family's farm was and where the actual Bunny Man attacks took place and was unsettled by the proximity! It's worth noting that after my grandfather died, there were no more Bunny Man sightings. And that's all I'll say about that.

When I turned eighteen and started working at MTV, I was in the fortunate position to travel a lot. In every single town I traveled to, I'd go out of my way to find a local bookstore or gift shop and pick up a book on local tall tales and legends. Some of these books are ghost stories. Some are about monsters. Other are about local characters who did horrible things or miraculous things or were just so weird people can't stop talking about them. I remember doing an interview during those MTV years and explaining this practice. I told the reporter that I wanted to be able to drive cross-country with my kids and have a story for every single stop we made.

And that has pretty much come true! It's something I still do when I travel, and I hope it's something my children will continue someday.

What are the stories and legends about your town?

If you haven't found them yet, it might take a little poking and prodding, but they're there. Try looking for them when you travel, too. Knowing the legends of the place you visit adds a layer of mystery and possibility.

Why stay in a hotel when you could stay in a haunted B&B? Why go on a garden or home tour when you could go on a ghost tour? Why go to a regular ol' run-of-the-mill restaurant instead of a haunted restaurant where a ghost bartender throws glasses at unruly customers!?

Stories matter. Legends matter. Passing them down matters. Oral traditions are how we kept our history, our values, and our knowledge on how to stay alive.

Over the last year, George has become one of those kids who don't listen so well. And that's okay. I like her being a button pusher and a rule breaker, just not when it's dinnertime or bedtime. So, my husband started telling her about the Monster that lives in our woods. And how if she didn't listen well, or started throwing a fuss and screaming, the Monster would hear it.

My child promptly marched her butt outside and screamed out into the darkness:

"Hello, Monster. Are you okay? How you doin' tonight?"

I know she's gonna grow up and tell her kids about the Monster in the woods and the Bunny Man and the Claw on the water tower. These stories are her inheritance, passed down through generations of mischief makers.

The only way for a story to live forever is if you start telling it.

Simple Spells

Poetry Spells

Come to my arms, cruel and sullen thing; Indolent beast, come to my arms again...

—Charles Baudelaire, "Lethe" from *Flowers of Evil*, translated by George Dillon and Edna St. Vincent Millay

*T*he very first poem I ever learned was "The Owl and the Pussycat" in second grade. Aside from the awkwardness of having to get up in front of my peers and perform "Oh Lovely Pussy, Oh Pussy, my love, What a beautiful Pussy you are!" (even at seven, I knew what was up), I fell in love with the recitation. Words can paint a picture, tell a story, and impart a feeling. I practiced that poem in my room for hours, muttering it under my breath until it was committed to memory for all eternity.

My favorite poem of all time is "Witch Wife," by Edna St. Vincent Millay. I memorized that one the moment I first read it. It felt like it was written especially for me.

But when you delve into more of Millay's poetry, you happen

upon some *spellwork*. "First Fig" is a poem I love so much that I've used it on all my social media handles.

"My candle burns at both ends; it will not last the night; but ah, my foes, and oh, my friends—it gives a lovely light!"

She's justifying her manic behavior, giving the bird to her enemies, and delighting in this lovely light of her labor. It's a little thing you can chant to yourself when you're feeling over-whelmed, knowing that your work—any work—is good work. Whether you're scrubbing toilets at home, making big sales, or creating art, burning your candle at both ends is a gift. The exhaustion is a gift.

So much of magical thinking is about controlling the lens through which you see things.

When we think of spells in books or movies, they're lyrical. They rhyme. Sometimes they're in Latin or Greek. And there's a cadence to them that infuses power in those words. Words are the most powerful tool a human has!

How do you connect poetry and spellwork? Well, practitioners of Psalmic magic have pretty much figured it out. The Book of Psalms in the Bible is some of the most beautiful poetry that's ever been written. Some people read it like it's a story. Others put it to music—Coolio's "Gangsta's Paradise," anyone (Psalm 23)?

But practitioners of Psalmic magic understand that each verse is its own powerful spell, that words divined by God have meaning and intention. This started off as a medieval Jewish tradition, honoring the Old Testament. But the practice of using psalms as protection spells made its way to Europe, and eventually was brought over to Appalachia by way of immigrants.

Riddle me this, though. The Book of Psalms was not written in English. Before it made its way to our shores, it had been translated time and time again. So how do new words, freshly translated, hold the same power as words of a different language?

Intent is everything.

If you set your heart on the intention behind your words, they will be equally productive.

Here are some verses that have been used in spellwork:

Psalm 1: For the protection of pregnant women from premature delivery or dangerous confinement.

Psalm 10: To rid yourself of evil spirits.

Psalm 45 and 46: To make peace between a man and wife.

Psalm 56: To free yourself from bonds of passion and sensuality. (Sometimes it's just too much, ya know?)

Psalm 85: To regain a lost friendship.

Psalm 144 and 145: Say this psalm if you are troubled by ghosts.

Part of the joy of poetry in your spellwork is that it's easier to remember than prose. It's more fun to say (like "The Owl and the Pussycat"!). It rolls off the tongue. It becomes a linguistic gift you can present to other people. I have gifted a number of friends with this poetic spell and a jar of good salt upon the purchase of a new home:

> Bless with gifts from the Earth,
> Bring this home a brand-new birth,
> Bless the doorways and the sill,

Bring good fortune, bring goodwill.
Bless the lock and bless the key,
Fill with magick, So mote it be.

Pretty simple. But it's an easy thing to remember as you sprinkle salt in the corners of your new home.

I follow accounts on Instagram that post poetry every single day. Some of them are quite good. Some of them are a bit of a stretch. Some of them are downright terrible. But from time to time, you'll catch a poem that will live in your head forever as a mantra, and *those* are your spells. Some people like the formality of Shakespearean language. Edna St. Vincent Millay was certainly inspired by the romance of sonnets. Others like the verbal modernity of e. e. cummings, where the visual presentation of letters and words holds just as much importance as the language itself. Just try to tell me this isn't a love spell:

[i carry your heart with me (i carry it in]
by e. e. cummings

i carry your heart with me (i carry it in
my heart) i am never without it (anywhere
i go you go, my dear; and whatever is done
by only me is your doing, my darling)
i fear
no fate (for you are my fate, my sweet) i want
no world (for beautiful you are my world, my true)
and it's you are whatever a moon has always meant
and whatever a sun will always sing is you

here is the deepest secret nobody knows
(here is the root of the root and the bud of the bud
and the sky of the sky of a tree called life; which grows
higher than soul can hope or mind can hide)
and this is the wonder that's keeping the stars apart

i carry your heart (i carry it in my heart)

Recite that while you braid a lock of your lover's hair into your own. Now, while on the topic of love spells? Our queen goth girl Emily Dickinson wrote a doozy! Recite this while cutting a flower to give to your beloved:

With a Flower

I hide myself within my flower,
That wearing on your breast,
You, unsuspecting, wear me too—
And angels know the rest.

I hide myself within my flower,
That, fading from your vase,
You, unsuspecting, feel for me
Almost a loneliness.

Writing and reading poetry to express a desire or call something to action is an innate practice. Think of how many people fill up spiral notebooks with horrible poetry in their teens and early adulthood. Why do we do that? Think about it. Why do human beings write poems? Is it to comfort ourselves? Is it a signal to others who might be feeling the same way? Is it to record a moment we want to remember for good or bad, just to remind us that we were alive?

The most impactful poetry is the stuff that addresses our innermost insecurities, but also our innermost strengths. So, figure out if you're the kind of person who is drawn to nature in poetry. Figure out if you're the kind of person who likes a lusty, bawdy rhyme. Perhaps you're the kind of person who wants a biblical passage for strength. Or maybe a song lyric works for you. And write, write, write, write, write!

Open your grimoire, where you can scribble your rhymes and reasonings and keep them like secrets.

I used to do coffee shop poetry slams with my goth friends in high school. And while I loved the performative nature of those poems, I also know the deep power of a poem that is kept to yourself. It is not made for anyone other than you.

And if you prefer not to exercise your writing ability, be the collector of words. Read one poem a day. Write down or rip out those poems that speak to your soul.

Regardless of which method you use to accumulate your poetry spells, tuck them away in anticipation of the day when you will need them (try a nightstand drawer, or tape one to your bathroom mirror, or stuff a few in your glove compartment). Forget about them. Let the universe surprise you when they tumble out at exactly the moment you need them. Because we're all going to face the same things in our life: grief, love, loss, and bliss. If we can use words to power us through those moments, we will have harnessed real magic.

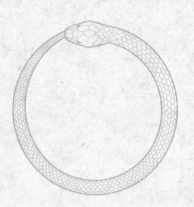

6

NO BEIGE HOMES

or the winter months of the great lockdown of 2020–21, Jeffrey, Gus, George, and I hunkered down in the Outer Banks of North Carolina. Years ago, we'd bought a ramshackle fixer-upper, and the house had recently weathered an aggressive series of storms and hurricanes. So, I did what I always do when I need help quieting my brain: I started renovating.

I was reeling from the realization we all were having: the hard, painful reality of being mortal as loss became an everyday occurrence. Like most Americans, we lost people we loved during that stagnant year. I printed out obituaries and tucked them in notebooks. There were no funerals, no memorials. Just words on paper to finalize the lives of our friends. During this time, I looked at our own children. Sweet Gus, with his love of Elvis and Minecraft, my brilliant George and her uncanny ability to curse like a fifty-year-old trucker. What would they read about us after

we were gone? What would be *our* words on the page? What
would be their inheritance? Whatever it ended up being, I hoped
it would be bold and colorful.

These thoughts led to a string of sleepless nights, while I
stayed up painting the dated 1980s kitchen cabinets a high-gloss
maritime blue. Using one of those Home Depot resurfacing kits, I
Cinderella-ed the stained laminate countertop into faux marble.
The process had been a long—and frankly, damn successful—one.
Anyone who says you can't put lipstick on a pig is wrong. This
beach kitchen was the ugliest kind of sow, but I'd done her up just
enough that she looked respectable. Jeffrey couldn't handle the
countertop, though. He still chuckles every time he sees it, saying,
"It looks like a high school drama department set."

Exactly, darling! And that's why I love it. Because I *am* a
drama department kid. Perhaps that's why I love the fixer-upper
in general. With its popcorn ceilings and frayed Berber carpet,
it's a throwback to the houses of my childhood. I don't need it to
be high end or modern. I don't need the marble to be real. I just
need to be able to sprawl out like a cat in a triangle of sunshine
on the floor with my children nearby and feel as if this house has
always been there. I need to feel as if it has always been my home
and always will be a part of our family. I love its dated architecture and familiar layout of clearly defined rooms—none of this
"common room" nonsense that's become fashionable in the last
couple of decades.

The homes of my childhood were ripe with terrible and very
specific color choices. But that's how you differentiated your house
from your best friend's house. In Virginia, everyone pretty much
had the same floor plan: it was either a split level or a center-stair
colonial.

There were formal rooms that were awash in Laura Ashley pastels, or earthy greens and golds, and in Northern Virginia, the colonial red, white, and blue variations were commonplace. *Brick and navy. Rose and Carolina blue.* Guest bathrooms boasted loud wallpaper and toilet seat covers made of the same carpet as the floor mat. Mauve. Baby pink. Ocean blue.

Is this what my fixation with old houses was based on? Color? My friend Erica's home had a 1960s color palette, with a neon floral couch that I tried to buy from her parents when I left for New York. I recall blue as the predominate color at my friend Ashley's house, the site of all our bitchin' pool parties. I painted my own bedroom sage green, a shade that was all the rage in the late 1990s.

Somewhere along the way, the tidal wave of home improvement and real estate television shows convinced everyone that the value of a home was in its resell price point. That you should be thinking of the next buyer, even while living in the home yourself. And that neutral was the only way to appear upscale and get a good price for your home. To this I scream with fury, *Bullshit!*

We have been conditioned to live in a world of pale gray and contractor's beige. It's dystopian. Ask any human out there what their favorite color is and only the most emo of creatures will say gray. As for beige? No one. Literally not one human will say beige. So why do we do this to ourselves?

The beach house is a double split-level of sorts, and when we bought it, wouldn't you know? It had all beige walls. Tall and skinny, it has an entry-level sand room where the washer and dryer hang out, a level of tiny bedrooms and bathrooms with dated fixtures and hollow wood doors, another level with a wood-paneled family room and kitchen, and then a crow's nest. The splittest of split-levels. So, it was while lying on this very carpeted beach house floor and feeling a physical tug for home that I could not suffer the beige for one moment longer.

I'd once seen an ad for an interior designer on the internet that said, "Go into your closet. Look at your favorite outfits. Look at what you look best in. And then decorate your home the way you'd decorate yourself." Well, anyone who knows Jeffrey and me understands that our closet is a sea of moody Addams Family black. His leather jackets sit squarely across from my witchy frocks, and our farm uniforms of black Carhartt thermals mingle together atop a dresser that houses our various many-pocketed black work pants.

So, while every other house on the tiny strip of Atlantic oceanfront was painted in either depressing tan shades or in perky nautical blues and pastel yellows, I hoisted myself on a huge extension ladder, got myself a spray gun, and painted the vaulted ceilings and walls of the entire interior a deep, intimidating charcoal. I stayed on that ladder, risking life and limb, to replace the brass chandeliers that had been corroded by decades of sea air, high humidity, and God knows what the previous renters had left in the ether. I put up fabulous mid-century lights and worried that I was becoming Catherine O'Hara in *Beetlejuice*, converting a perfectly quaint home into my mystical cavern of modernity. The shabby-chic kitchen table that had come with the house was a light and passive maple, with chunky farmhouse legs. So naturally I sanded the hell out of it, flipped it upside-down, and knocked the legs off with a hammer. While my children slept, it became a dark mahogany with mid-century hairpin legs at each corner. But because I'm not a total monster, I also painted the bathrooms a cheery 1960s dusty-pink color. Even the grumpiest of us girls have a super femme streak we let show from time to time. Beach Goth is a vibe that has no resale value. It is as niche as they come. But it has absolute lifestyle value. My kids will remember the cave and how we projected disco lights across the ceiling at night.

Our home sweet home, Mischief Farm, is also a palette of deep black paint and distressed wood. Inside is a mix of wood beams and moody fatigue-green walls. The dark wash of shadow does something to a home. Suddenly, the walls disappear entirely, and your eye is swiftly drawn to the windows and views. It's the way a movie theater is designed; the eye is drawn to the light of the screen while everything else dissolves into the periphery. Scuffs and imperfections soften into a blur, and the bright glow of dawn and midday sun and dramatic sunset take over each room.

Do not be afraid of the dark rooms. They only serve to make the light more apparent.

So, our beach fixer-upper became the sister-house to our goth farm. In the process, I created order. I had control. I had a to-do list that kept my brain from wandering into murkier territory. And that was worth losing a few dollars on the resale price.

Candle Magic

Despite what our modern society would have you believe, the Witch within you is not dangerous, but protective. She is not frivolous, but exceedingly accurate and trustworthy.

—Laurie Cabot, Witchcraft High Priestess and
civil rights activist

*A*s long as we are talking about color, it makes sense to go ahead and dive into candle magic. Full disclosure: this is *my* preferred method of magic. There are lots of different kinds of witches out there—kitchen witches, garden witches, crystal witches, solitary witches, green witches, hearth witches, sex witches (yup!)—and my own personal belief is that it's good to know a little of each, if for no other reason than to commune with the other spirited creatures. For me, there has always been a constant tug from all things flame related. I like my magic to be active. I can watch a candle burn down or a scrap of paper turn to ash. The same way some people know they are auditory learners, or kinesthetic learners who need to do the activity to retain it, or visual learners, you will innately know which method of spell casting is best for you. I need a strong visual, and there is nothing more mysterious and powerful than the flame. I'm drawn to the languid, swirling motion of smoke, the communicative motion of flame with its range of heat and color, and the physical transformation of solid material into cinders.

And it makes sense that I would be so drawn to this element. Since childhood, I have been hearing stories of my paternal grandmother. Dorothy was a woman I didn't really know. I can count the number of times I remember seeing her on one hand. I heard about her while sitting at the feet of other adults, pretending to play. She had too many children. Poverty was a common visitor. She was a housekeeper for a fancy family in a neighboring town. *But*, Dorothy knew magic.

The family shared vivid stories about her healing powers. One involved a coworker of my grandfather who had been tarring a roof and had lava-hot material poured on him; another, a little kid in the family getting burned badly by a cigarette. In both instances, I was told that rather than seek medical attention right away, Dorothy was called in to whisper in the injured person's ear. No one heard what she was saying or could understand what her hands were doing. But the burn would dissipate. A light scab would fall off, leaving no scar. The ability to combat fire was wild to me! And obviously, I wanted to know how it was done. Instead, I was told that knowledge can only be passed down from female to male or male to female, and so the fantasy of this grandmother I didn't really know gifting me her knowledge was dead in the water.

At the advent of the internet, I started doing some digging on my own. Ask Jeeves was the Google of its time, and I would stay up late entering queries into the search engine.

How to heal burns? Spell to heal burns? Burn magic? Folk magic for burns?

It was a fruitless search until 2010 when Jeffrey, Gus, and I moved into our little log cabin in the Hudson Valley. I remember exactly where I was sitting, in the window seat of my kitchen, when I stumbled upon a website that described the sacred—and very secretive—practice of Appalachian Granny Magic.

The 1700s saw the arrival of Irish and Scottish settlers in the Appalachian Mountains, and much the same way Christianity was blended with African traditions in Haiti to establish Voodoo, the Europeans brought their faith to these hills and combined their beliefs with the knowledge of the Native American communities. The resources of the cities didn't exist, so everyone was expected to be part farmer, part doctor, part preacher. Some folks had a talent for finding water, some for healing ailments, some for love and protection spells, and some for talking the fire out of burns. For the most part, spells were a prayer to God uttered three times, and after each time the practitioner made the sign of the cross.

It means a lot to me that this was a culture where witches were not persecuted or killed. This skill that my grandma Dorothy had was considered a gift. And so, it had been passed down for hundreds of years, from mother to son and father to daughter and aunt to nephew and so on, until my grandmother died about a decade ago. I thought the magic was lost. She had only two sons, and she certainly didn't pass along the knowledge to my father.

Imagine my surprise when during my pregnancy with George, I received a phone call from a second cousin, a male family member who had been given the gift by his own mother, my grandmother's sister. He was ready to share the knowledge with me.

"Don't write it down," he warned me. "Don't share it casually. We've traced this back in our family over 240 years."

And so that's all I'm gonna share! If someone tells you to respect a gift, you do. My husband, the ultimate skeptic, had his reservations. But he has been on the receiving end of some of this healing and now sends anyone with a burn to me.

So clearly, I feel connected to the flame. Evidence suggests that man has used fire for around one million years, campfires leading to torches and then candles and lanterns. Fire still helps us tap into the magic of shedding light in the dark.

We've all practiced a little candle magic. Maybe you've lit a votive in a church, or set out candles for a romantic dinner, or, at the very least, stuck some birthday candles on a cake and sung. Candles can mark a ritual or put a spell into motion, so set your intention and light a fire.

Now, the color of your candles is just as important as it is in your home. We have a subconscious reaction to specific colors. Your response to a color is anchored in *your* experience of the world and the culture that you live in. Here's a key to the significance of certain candle colors in Western cultures, but if for you crimson is the color of truth, then paint the town red.

White candles can be lit to call to the lunar and goddess energies. You can use them for purification, healing, and harmony, and to mark new beginnings. White candles are a powerful tool for meditation, peace, and gratitude, and to help calm your mind. And white candles are a great stand-in if you don't have the color candle you need at a particular time.

Black candles can activate protection spells and reverse curses. They can clear negativity and bad habits or stop an unhealthy cycle or situation. Lighting one of these dark beauties will banish all that toxic energy that can swirl into our lives.

Red candles channel the power of Mars and invoke passion and lust, of course. They can also be linked to an urge to survive and a sense of determination. You can light a red candle to help with confidence, willpower, strength, and bravery. And not only will they help attract a romantic partner, but good luck, too.

Pink candles foster love, self-love, and compassion. Light one to deepen empathy, connection, and intimacy and to strengthen and heal relationships, or burn one to bring joy and promote happiness.

Yellow candles can be lit to help usher in new ideas, to gain clarity, or to help open your mind—allowing focus, learning, and intellectual pursuit. Light a yellow candle and open a book from your witchy library.

Blue is the color of peace, serenity, and wisdom. Light a blue candle to help you connect to your higher self. There's the added benefit of improving memory, finding spiritual healing, and enhancing your ability to communicate, including prophetic dreams and creative inspiration.

Green candles evoke abundance in all earthly things and are

lit for prosperity and good luck. If you forgot the collard greens on New Year's Day, light a green candle to bring in the money. Or, if you're practicing earth and plant magic, a green candle can help you connect with Mother Nature.

Brown candles represent the earth and are a grounding force, promoting peace and neutrality. They can help you find lost objects, establish balance, and build trust.

Purple is the color of the divine. If you want to harness your psychic power and open your third eye, burn a purple candle. These can also be used for divination, deepening your spiritual awareness, and strengthening your intuition to gain wisdom and uncover secrets.

Orange candles marry the intellectual energy of yellow candles and the passion of red ones, beckoning in creativity, abundance, and passion. They can help you in affairs where quick action and a clear mind are needed, and can be used to invite a sense of playfulness and joy into your life.

Gold draws on male energy or the energy of the Sun God. A gold candle can be burned to bring confidence, success, prosperity, and enlightenment.

Silver is a special color for Wiccans; these candles represent the Goddess. Similarly to purple candles, they will help you connect to the divine, strengthening your astral and female energy, and to lean into your intuitive side, helping you open up to telepathy and clairvoyance.

I gift packages of multicolored candles to my curious friends, giving them the building blocks they need to manifest on their own. And while color alone is a powerful way to focus your intentions, personalizing your ritual tools and being creative with your process is just as important. There's no real guidebook for this, just accumulated suggestions from other spiritual practitioners. But here are a few of the habits I've picked up.

+ Carve a word or intention into your candle, giving it very specific directions.
+ Add other elements with similar intentions to your candle. A good example is a pink candle for self-love. Ylang-ylang essential oil is known for reducing stress and fear and promoting self-esteem, while rose quartz is the stone connected to healing the heart. Anoint the candle with oil and place it on your altar with the rose quartz. Focus your energy.
+ I like to write my intentions on bay leaves and light them on fire from my candles, dropping them in an old copper pot while they continue burning. The act of making a prayer or a wish and keeping it a secret is important. So much of church and religion is performative. A secret and sacred communication between you and your God is a healthy way to know your intentions are pure and not for an audience.
+ The pin drop! I really like this one. Take a candle and, as you say your intention aloud, run a pin through it. Then light the candle and let it burn down. If your flame goes out or the pin stays in the candle? It ain't happening, babe. But if your candle drops the pin as it burns down? Your manifestation will occur.

II

Into a Dark
Wood

7

MAKING FRIENDS WITH GHOSTS

here comes a time in everyone's life when they must venture away from the safety of home and make their own way. I was twenty-one during the first season of *One Tree Hill*. Right out of the gate I was a rowdy youth, living above the infamous Firebelly Bar, steps from the equally infamous Cape Fear River. The bar in question had been the scene of a fight in which Vince Vaughn got arrested and Steve Buscemi had been stabbed in the face. Coming from New York City, it was odd to think that this sleepy little coastal town could be more dangerous than the concrete wilds of the Lower East Side. But the story about that tabloid-fodder bar fight was one of the first things I'd heard when I moved to town. *Watch out for that place! The locals get ornery there!* So naturally, when an apartment opened up two floors above the bar, I signed over first and last month's rent and bought a scary 1960s French painting in an antiques store down the street to christen the pad.

But the hype didn't really pan out. The Firebelly was just a bar. They served cheap tacos and not very strong drinks. The danger I'd been so drawn to soon wore off, and Firebelly turned into a convenient basement where I'd meet the crew after long days of filming and then crawl up to bed as the sun came up.

There was a tug on my heart to find a real home. And so, one brisk winter day, I went for a walk through the colorful historic district of Wilmington. I saw "For Rent" signs sprinkled over the various blocks I explored. But it wasn't until I reached Nun Street, right on the fringe of the "safe" part of town, that I found my gem. There were sister houses, two-story Victorians, mirror images of one another. One sat completely vacant and open to the elements. The other sat bland in her beige-ness, overrun with neglected azaleas and oleander, with a "For Rent" sign propped up in the front window. She had a little front porch, which I climbed onto so as to peer into the windows. I saw wood floors and a fireplace and parlor doors and twelve-foot ceilings, and I was hooked. I called the number on the sign and told the landlord, "I want it."

"Don't you want to see inside first?" he asked. It wouldn't have mattered. This old lady of a house was mine and nothing could have steered me away. I moved in a week later and from day one, I knew this house was *alive*.

We were moving in furniture when I met my neighbor, Rabbi George. I found him on my back deck, feeding an abandoned cat while my father, brother, and boyfriend-at-the-time carted in chairs and beds and dressers. He looked formal, in a dress shirt, slacks, and yarmulke, small wire-framed glasses highlighting his Carolina-blue eyes. A silver beard disguised his true age; he could have been forty or seventy. George introduced himself and motioned over the fence to his yard, where there was a stunning Secret Garden tucked behind a tidy brick home. From my little abused sandlot of a yard, his space was like something out of a storybook. An oasis you peek at through a keyhole.

"Feel free to come pick flowers whenever you like," he told me in his gentle Southern drawl, and I knew we'd be friends right away. After he left, I returned inside to help the boys and told them about my new friend. An hour or so later I went to the bathroom, and all hell broke loose. I was completely taken aback when I emerged to find all the boys outside the door, bowed up as if I'd been in there with someone.

"Did that George guy come back?"

"What? No, why?"

They went to examine the back door. It was bolted shut.

"We heard a man in here!" Whoever they had heard had a deep voice, and they were adamant that they had heard him talking with me by the bathroom.

"Maybe it was an echo," I suggested. They all protested.

"We all heard it."

There was a voice in the house, but to whom did it belong?

I spent the next few weeks nesting, planting the garden, and turning the crooked old house into a cozy den of eccentricity. My father was an antiques dealer, and we'd been raised to have an eye for oddities—or treasures, as we called them. The home quickly filled up with Victorian odds and ends and taxidermy.

What I couldn't find in junk shops and antiques stores I built, including a bed and a bar and a couch for the library. And that is when I began to notice a rather odd occurrence. Anytime I embarked upon a home improvement project, strange happenings began in the house. Radios were turned off and on. I would hear the sound of the front door opening and closing. I'd find candles lit. And somehow, I was not the least bit afraid. My brothers and boyfriend on the other hand, were being terrorized.

One day, the landlord, Tom, dropped by while I was planting lantana along the stone wall that lined the sidewalk. He was a breezy kind of guy—loose Tommy Bahama shirts, sandals, sometimes a cat resting on his shoulders. Eccentric without trying to be. "Lemme ask you something, Tom. This place haunted?"

His face! I honestly couldn't tell if he most certainly *had* heard something about a ghost or if he just thought I was nuts. But he looked at me sideways and said, "Who told you that?"

He said he'd never heard of anything from any of the previous tenants. Okay, Tom.

So, I went to Rabbi George.

Our conversation started off with me asking for tips on plants, and he was very complimentary about the improvements I'd made on the place. George had planted cherry blossom trees in front of both our houses years before, and that spring I was dizzy with the scent of the luscious pink petals that swirled on our sidewalk.

I'd never had a front porch growing up, just that grand maple tree I'd hide up in. So front porch culture was foreign and exciting for me—neighbors chatting it up, taking in the beauty and small pleasures of the day. But I was still a newbie and had no chill. So that day on my front porch I blurted out, "Is this house haunted?"

George gave me a knowing look.

I was living in Hester Donnelly's house. Local legend. Creator of the art museum in Wilmington. Notorious party-thrower. Incredibly active ghost.

Hester was born in 1912 and lived her whole life at 212 Nun

Street. She died in 1992, about a decade before I moved in. She had no siblings, no children, no family to speak of, save a distant cousin or two. But she wasn't a woman without connections. As a girl, her life was forever changed when she began taking art classes from an eccentric middle-aged woman who had moved to town in 1922, Elisabeth Chant.

Miss Chant, as her pupils called her, was a wild character. The daughter of a ship captain, her claim to fame was that she had sailed the seven seas before she was seven years old. In my imagination, she resembled Pippi Longstocking, with her braids and wild stories. Miss Chant's father wanted her to become a lady and get a good education, so he planted the family down in Minneapolis. But bohemia had already been infused in young Miss Chant's blood, and she found herself drawn to a passionate artistic community that was emerging in the area. Being a talented painter, she set up a successful salon in the Twin City with her closest friend. It was seemingly bliss. But a few hard years hit Miss Chant, and in quick succession, her father and best friend died.

Those losses were only two months apart. The grief sent Miss Chant into a spiral. She claimed she could communicate with spirits and shunned typical Christian practices, and so her family had her arrested, then committed to a mental institution in 1917. She was kept there for three years.

Upon her release, Miss Chant knew she needed a change of scenery, so she wrote various city councils offering her services as an art teacher. When Wilmington responded, she hopped a train and made the move—a brilliant decision on her part. Everyone knows that in the South, we don't commit the "crazy," we celebrate them. The local paper recorded her much anticipated arrival, and it is said she disembarked the train wearing a Chinese robe with her hair in braided buns at her ears. I think this is exactly how a grown-up Pippi would wear her hair.

It seems the parents in town either didn't know about Miss Chant's little stay in the sanatorium or they didn't care, because everyone—including the Donnellys—sent their children to her. The most famous of her students, Claude Howell, is a favorite of mine.

The very practices that had alarmed Miss Chant's family back in Minnesota delighted the Wilmington crowd. She talked to spirits? Magnificent. She declared herself a Druid? How delightful! Over the years Miss Chant exposed her pupils not only to the wonders of art, but to the cultures of the wider world.

Hester was dazzled. And in turn, Miss Chant saw a protégé. They hosted art fairs together, established art councils, and created museums and more learning opportunities for the students of Wilmington, young and old alike. They were independent women who enjoyed being less than "normal." And when Miss Chant died in 1947, Hester picked up that artistic baton and ran with it. The modern-day Cameron Art Museum began as a gallery that Hester established with the belongings that Miss Chant had left to her, including paintings and trunks of letters and mementos.

By this point, Hester's father had died in a tragic incident with a car while he was out walking the family Boston terrier, and her mother had remained bedridden in what would later be my bedroom for years. Hester could have easily spiraled, but instead she made art her life's work, preserving Miss Chant's memory and teaching a love of art to an entirely new generation of Wilmingtonians.

"Did you meet Hester when you moved in?" I'd asked Rabbi George.

"Oh no," he replied. "I'd met her long before. At the Azalea

Festival." For those who don't know, the Azalea Festival is the biggest party of the year down in Wilmington, full of princesses and parades. "I'd always liked art," Rabbi George continued. "And so, I was walking down the alleyway next to the post office, and there was a sign that said 'Art Gallery.'" Hester had indeed founded the first year-round art museum with her friend Virginia McQueen at 3 Post Office Alley. Claude Howell, who had been growing in fame, was bothered that he had nowhere to show his art in his own hometown. So, his art class friends showed up and ran the gallery from 1958 to 1962.

"I went in and there were two women sitting there, and it was real dark," my neighbor recalled. "All of a sudden this bellowing voice said, 'Come on in.' I thought, *Oh my goodness, what is this?* And there was Hester the Jester, with a French beret on her head."

"Was she happy to see you when you moved in next door?"

Rabbi George laughed at my question. "She didn't like me at all! I'd bought the house from a couple who were getting a divorce. And she liked the couple. And so, I don't know, somehow in her mind she thought if I didn't buy the house, the couple would stay together."

Rabbi George moved to Nun Street in 1973, and every week he'd cut Hester's grass and do odd jobs around her property, trying to be a good neighbor. Back in the seventies, Nun Street had been home to the Cumber clan, a family of racist ne'er-do-wells who let the homeless sleep on their porches for a fee. Across the street from them was a prominent brothel where local politicians and businessmen would send their illegitimate children to be raised. Rabbi George told stories of the limos driving up, money being passed out of the windows, and kids hollering after the departing vehicles. It painted a grim picture. So he began getting together with a few other residents once a month to rehab the historic homes and encourage other neighbors to join the newly formed Residents of Old Wilmington.

Hester was having none of it, according to George. "She would have her Christmas party and invite me. But then spend the whole time saying, 'I'm not speaking to him, but he's my neighbor so I have to have him over.'"

I was wildly curious about these parties of Hester's, because it seemed they were continuing well into my tenure in the Nun Street house. There was a night early on where my boyfriend and I had been working odd hours, and so we were having trouble falling asleep. When the sound of music floated up from the parlor below at two o'clock in the morning, we lay there not moving a muscle. It was big-band brass music sounding crackly, like it was from a phonograph. The moment we turned to look at each other it faded away, but it had been unmistakably there. And that wouldn't be the last time the ghost party happened.

"She'd have a lot of people, a lot of them older, like the Claude Howell type. Local artists. Theater-type people, and then just some regular people like me," Rabbi George recalled. "People sat around and talked, and she had simple hors d'oeuvres. I heard her telling someone that cucumber sandwiches were her famous thing to fix, and if she didn't have it at a party, people would be very disappointed." It's a funny visual to me, rough and abrasive Hester fussing with cute little tea party sandwiches. "She was just so proud of it!" Rabbi George said.

Hester had been a local celebrity, directing and performing in productions at the stunning historic theater, Thalian Hall. Members of Thalian Hall recounted how she could be heard audibly groaning or heckling during particularly amateur performances. As she got older and became a local icon like Miss Chant before her, Hester established a reputation for two things: the beret she wore every day, and her very deep voice, which was renowned for being less than tactful.

The more I learned, the closer I felt to Hester. I'd been throwing parties of my own, filling the front parlor with artists again. I love that she cultivated community and had a sharp tongue and an authoritative voice.

EVENTUALLY, GEORGE HAD WON HESTER OVER. THEY'D BEEN neighbors for almost twenty years, and as Hester got older and grew sick, George would bring in her newspaper every morning and keep her yard in good shape. When she died, a distant relative asked him if he would be a pallbearer. After the funeral, no one really knew what to do with Hester's estate. Again, Rabbi George was contacted and asked if he could help sell her belongings. Hester had been a huge lover of literature and had shelves and shelves full of first-edition books. George called Mr. Daughtry from the bookstore downtown (the very same bookstore where I would hide out on *One Tree Hill*, and where Michelle Williams was rumored to have camped out before me while filming *Dawson's Creek*).

Mr. Daughtry took what he could, but there was still a great deal left over. The woman handling the estate was emphatic. "Please. Take anything you want."

There had been a nice bookcase right at the entrance of Hester's house. "And so," Rabbi George told me, "I went back when I got off work. It was winter and it was dark early. And I'm going through this bookcase and had gotten some of the first editions. And then at the top of the stairs I heard this voice. I saw two bright things that were like eyeballs."

"Oh Jesus, George!" I winced.

"I looked up and heard, 'Haven't you taken enough?' in a deep voice like Hester's. I . . . I got out of that house as fast as I could." (It's worth noting that the entire time I lived in Hester's house, George politely declined anytime I invited him to come inside.) Even after Rabbi George shared his rather ominous story, I still wasn't scared of my ghost or my haunted rental house. But once my six-month lease was up, I decided I needed to buy a place. *One Tree Hill* was always on the verge of being cancelled, but I had a very "Field of Dreams" mindset—*If you build it, they will come* turned into *If I buy a house, the show will stay.* I set out scouring the neighborhood for available historic homes. But the morning I was to go out with a real estate agent, Hester's house would not let me get ready. The electricity kept flickering, and the water would turn back and forth between ice cold and hot. Hester was dropping hints.

I looked at every property for sale in town and found something wrong with all of them. Defeated, I came back to Hester's house and sat down on the couch. A warm feeling came over me as the obvious answer became clear. *Why don't I buy this house?* I called the landlord, who then called the owner, who was living in a different state, and an hour later the deal was done. It was fate.

As official owner of 212 Nun Street, I proudly renovated, always with signs of my ghost roommate following. I didn't have aunts and uncles, but I had this adopted relative. And just like Elisabeth Chant, I became known as the young lady who talked to spirits.

I don't know if I would have been as bold about venturing out into the community if I didn't have Hester as my guide. My search for her led me to my neighbors, the theater community, the Cameron Art Museum, the public library, and the Hannah Block

Community Arts Center. Hester lived this big, full life in a tiny town, paving the way for me to do the same. There would be no Mischief Farm or *Rural Diaries* if there hadn't been the mystery of Hester Donnelly and Nun Street.

Once I'd earned my stripes as an accepted member of the neighborhood, elderly neighbors up the street invited me over for an ice cream social and showed me a watercolor painting Hester had done, with the newspaper clipping of her obituary taped to the back. In it, she is described as "gruff, and wonderful." What an absolute legend.

Parties and Potions

There is so much magic in medicine making, and learning to listen to the plants you feel drawn to makes the process much more personal and powerful.

—Spencre L. R. McGowan, from *Blotto Botany: A Lesson in Healing Cordials and Plant Magic*

*R*abbi George shared this memory with me: "Hester took white bread, and she would cut the crust off. She'd take something that was round, and she'd get like two round pieces out of the white bread. Then she'd put mayonnaise on. And then she would put cucumber, the pepper and then some paprika, and that was her famous appetizer."

What I wouldn't give to have attended just one of Hester Donnelly's famous parties! The idea that this abrasive, creative woman hypnotized her circle of friends with a simple cucumber tea sandwich is such a perfect visual. I have spent countless hours in that kitchen, hunched over the same island countertop, gazing out of the same wavy-glassed windows. There was a little something extra in those sandwiches, and I wish I knew what incantations Hester was muttering as she punched out bread rounds and sprinkled the spices.

I'd never been a party thrower before I lived in Hester's house. My teenage birthdays were all joint affairs with friends at their homes. All I had to do was show up. College wasn't much better. Maybe a night out? I honestly don't remember any of those occasions. But suddenly, with a home to call my own, I became the princess of parties, goddess of galas, sorceress of soirees. Had Hester enchanted me?

I made menus and designed décor. I had playlists and ice sculptures and hired palm readers and magicians. Themed evenings stretched well into the wee hours, and I wouldn't hit the pillow until the soft orange of dawn peeked through the curtains. There were birthdays and Thanksgivings and hurricane parties. But most importantly, there were the Halloween parties. I can most definitely say that this was the chapter of my life where my debaucherous streak was practiced and perfected. And there is no one from my life back then who is at all surprised that my husband and I recently launched a liquor line.

MF Libations is my offering to the party that is life. Whereas Hester crafted her sandwiches, my husband and I spent months tinkering with our partners Eral and Cliff and the gang at the local Vale Fox Distillery here in the Hudson Valley. We wanted to make something that provided an experience of Mischief Farm. But how do you bottle a feeling? That's exactly what potion making is all about!

We made a list of our favorite activities here on the farm.

Jeffrey's obviously centered on all things fire related (Is it any wonder he married a burn healer?): sawing up dead trees, chopping wood, sharpening hatchets, knife making, bonfires, fireplace fires, making kindling.

It was a no-brainer that the liquid we needed to match Jeffrey's intentions had to carry that feeling of fire. Eral suggested we try a tea from a local business, Harney & Sons. Lapsang Souchong tea originated in the Wuyi Mountains of China and is one of the oldest black teas, getting its distinctive taste from a process that involves smoking the leaves over a pine fire. It was perfect. We decided to infuse it into a spicy rye whiskey and played with ratios and the amount of time the tea sat with the spirit. Thus, our Bonfire Rye was born. A potion that could be shipped and shared all over the world.

Now, there are two ways I like to use this liquid, one hot and one cold.

My husband uses the Bonfire Rye to make me a classic Penicillin. I don't know that I have ever ordered this drink in a bar or restaurant or underground members-only club. But, as the name insinuates, this is a drink that is medicine for my soul when made by my person. He knows when I've had a trying day. The same way a cup of perfectly made coffee can be a love potion each and every morning, a well-timed nightcap is full of intention. There's a little prep work, as this recipe requires a honey-ginger syrup. So much of witchcraft was labeled as such because laymen didn't understand the healing properties of basic ingredients. But skilled medicine women have known the importance of both honey and ginger for ages. Honey has been credited with everything from healing burns to improving memory, curing basic coughs and colds, and fighting cancer. Ginger is best known for its assistance in digestion, but it's also credited with getting rid of headaches and fighting heart and lung disease. This is a syrup you should always have on hand as a dutiful kitchen witch.

To make honey-ginger syrup, you will need:

1 cup honey
1 peeled finger of ginger root (approximately 6 inches)
1 cup water

Place those three simple ingredients in a saucepan over high heat and bring to a boil. Reduce to medium heat and let lightly bubble for another 5 minutes. Let the concoction cool and pour into a mason jar. Put it in the fridge overnight, and in the morning you can strain it and rebottle it. Now, on to the Penicillin recipe!

Get yourself:

2 oz Bonfire Rye
3/4 oz lemon juice
3/4 oz honey-ginger syrup

Add each element to a shaker with ice, and give it an aggressive shake to toss off any of the complications of the day. Pour into a glass and garnish with a lemon twist, candied ginger, or maybe a makeout.

The other way I love our Bonfire Rye is in a hot toddy. We live in an area that can be brutal in winter, and we have kids who bring home every cough and cold imaginable. So, I like to get ahead of all the ailments and keep hot toddies in my nightly routine. This drink has mostly the same elements as the Penicillin. Put a hefty spoonful of local honey in a mug. Boil some water and pour into the mug to dissolve the honey. Add the lemon juice and Bonfire Rye. Stir together and breathe in that steam for a minute.

The other "potion" we created with MF Libations was our Blackberry Gin. My list of Mischief Farm activities was very different from Jeffrey's. The things that lit me up revolved around gardening and harvesting, picking dandelions for wine, vegetables and kale from the garden, peaches from the tree planted by our predecessors, and my berry patches. Our time on Mischief Farm has been a long ongoing experiment with canning and making pies and juicing, along with various other methods of preserving and enjoying the fruits of our labor. But it was when I discovered the practice of shrub making that I truly fell in love.

The week after our wedding, Jeffrey was already back in Georgia filming *The Walking Dead*. It was mid-October and I knew there was going to be a full moon that weekend. Last minute, I packed the kids up, and we went on a not-honeymoon to Salem, Massachusetts. We did the whole she-bang: ghost tours, museums, haunted restaurants. I geeked out when I discovered that Elvira was doing a fan convention in our hotel. It was a magical mini-adventure. In the last couple of hours of our trip, with George in a carrier attached to my back, we wandered in and out of shops until we stumbled across HausWitch Home + Healing. Historic and deeply intentional, it felt like a shop set up in the front parlor of the house belonging to the coolest witch you know. I spent an indulgent amount of time perusing the shelves and finally arrived at a little green book that had been continuing to catch my peripheral eye. *Blotto Botany* wasn't much larger than my hand, but packed inside was a treasure trove of recipes and herbal knowledge and fanzine artwork. The author, Spencre McGowan, dedicated an entire section to shrubs, vinegar-based tinctures traditionally used to preserve fruits so that they will last well into winter. Friends, I went home and started shrubbing every damn thing I could get my hands on. My fridge was lined with jars and repurposed bottles brimming with colorful and potent plant medicine. I have always had trouble regulating my pH balance, and vinegar was my standard go-to. But straight vinegar is certainly not without its pitfalls. Shrub-life became my daily routine.

When I explained all this to my partners at the distillery, they asked, "What's your favorite shrub?"

It was a no-brainer: blackberry. Of all the things I grow here, blackberries are my favorite. Everything about them, from their thorny brambles to their fairy-pink flowers and glossy black fruit, I find intoxicating. Eral and Cliff already knew I was partial to the botanical nature of gin, and their Vale Fox gin was a particular favorite of mine. Infused with rooibos tea—known for medicinal qualities that include cancer prevention and skin health, as well as the magical properties of rejuvenation and resiliency—it has a flowery essence and was the perfect thing to combine with our beloved blackberries.

Now I had the perfect ingredient to add to my shrubs!

Spencre has a recipe for a citrus shrub that goes beautifully with either our rye or our gin, and I have a shrub recipe that keeps me neck deep in blackberries all year long. You can mix 2 ounces of MF Blackberry Gin with 2 ounces of shrub and top off with whatever fizzy water you like best. Or use that shrub all by its lonesome and mix it with bubbly water or hot water to make an alcohol-free version. Place edible flowers or herbs in ice trays and make yourself some pretty cubes to toss into your elixirs.

Spencre McGowan's Blotto Botany—Meyer Lemon and Blood Orange Shrub

5 Meyer lemons
2 large blood oranges
1½ cups local honey
2 sprigs fresh rosemary or 1 cup fresh or dried holy basil
champagne or apple cider vinegar
1 half-gallon glass jar with lid

Gently scrub the lemons and oranges with warm water and cut into thin slices. Place in a glass jar along with honey and rosemary and muddle with a long wooden spoon. Completely cover with vinegar and cap tightly. I recommend putting a piece of fabric between the lid and jar to prevent sticking. Infuse on counter or in fridge for two weeks before straining.

Hilarie's Blackberry Shrub

Just so you know, you can sub out the berries and herbs and replace with any fruit and herbs you prefer. The point is to be creative and honor your own preferences! It's all about equal parts: one part fruit, one part liquid, one part sugar.

1½ cups blackberries
1½ cups sugar
1 cup vinegar (champagne, white or apple cider)
½ cup water
1 handful of herbs: mint, rose petals, sage, rosemary,
jasmine, hibiscus or whatever gets you excited

Some people like to use the cold method described above, where you muddle the fruit and sugar and let it rest in the fridge with the vinegar for 10 to 14 days. You can also use a hot method that more closely resembles the simple syrup process. Mash your fruit with the sugar in a stainless-steel pot over medium heat until the juices are released and bubbling. Add the vinegar, water, and herbs and let simmer for at least 20 minutes. Let cool, strain, and bottle the mixture, always remembering to put some cheesecloth or fabric between the container and lid. Once chilled, you can use this right away if you don't have two weeks to spare. The cold method probably keeps more of the antioxidants, but if you're an impulsive party thrower like Hester and me? *Double, double, toil and trouble. Fire burn and shrub doth bubble!*

PAPER MAIL

o any of you ever get that feeling of little shivers running up your neck? I do, especially when I receive paper mail. It's like feathers or whispers at the back of your ears. I don't know if anything makes me feel quite as loved as a letter being delivered to my home.

Obviously, we know that writing things down holds significant power. Out of all the creatures on the planet, we've been gifted with this magical ability to *record*—and therefore share—our innermost thoughts, our whims, our terrible poetry, and our feelings for one another. As a sentimental someone who has kept journals her entire life, I'm a firm believer in taking it one step further and indulging in the art of paper mail.

Look at it this way: paper mail is your opportunity to make another living, breathing person your human diary. In a world where email and text messages have taken over, there is romance to an honest-to-God paper letter. The time it takes to craft is part of that magic.

Writing paper mail is also an opportunity to show off handwriting—good or bad. I have been sucked in by the tiny typewriter handwriting of my dear friend and writing partner Nick Gray. And I love my husband's chicken scratch so much that we have used it as the font on the labels for our liquor business, MF Libations. Handwriting is like scent, unique to each human. Knowing a person's handwriting is proof of intimacy. I could see the handwriting of my classmates from thirty years ago and still absolutely be able to discern who wrote what.

The first mail I remember receiving was from a school-organized pen pal in second or third grade. The letters started coming from a little girl who went to school in a different state. And although for the life of me I cannot remember her name or where she was from, I remember how big I felt getting her notes. She continued to write me through the summer and at an age when I did not have very many friends, it meant a lot to me to hold a tangible note from another person. It felt like proof that I was cared for. I remember being very serious about my letters back to her. What color ink would I use? Should I draw a picture? Were stickers cool or not cool?!

When you get a little bit older, the letters turn into notes passed in class, folded into intricate patterns and stored in shoe boxes beneath the bed. It's embarrassing how many notes I have saved from middle and high school. And by embarrassing, I mean totally fucking awesome. Let's just hope my children never find them. I was lucky enough to go to a lot of camps and participate in theater as a kid, so I interacted with a number of people outside my school district. The only way we could really stay in touch was through paper letters. I didn't get my first email account until my senior year in high school. At that point, it was too late and my heart was set on old-school paper. I had amassed a serious collection of love letters, correspondence with mentors, as well as cards from girls I'd roomed with at Student Government retreats. Each of those letters is a little time capsule reminding me of slang we don't use anymore and moments that otherwise would have been lost to time.

Then when I got older and started working on *One Tree Hill*, paper mail really became a choice. I was a recluse living in an old haunted house, and I wanted my interactions with certain people to be deeply intentional. There is a commitment to writing a message down on paper. It takes days for that note to arrive, so it can't be something that is done in the heat of the moment. Otherwise, you might change your mind about how you're feeling a few minutes later. And the recipient could be receiving your wrath *days* after you've gotten over it!

No, paper mail was for deep, true feelings—good or bad.

The other remarkable thing about paper mail is that once you send it, you can't go back and reread it (unless you're some kind of psycho who writes out a separate draft just for keeps!). It's like live television: once it's done, it's done. You can't overthink it. You can't take it back. It's a commitment.

One of my favorite pen pals has been my hero, witchy author Alice Hoffman. I still can't believe our paths crossed and that she's written my name with her own hand! I think she thought me a curious girl at first, insisting on old-fashioned correspondence. But I'd loved *Practical Magic*, *The Red Garden*, and so many of her other books for decades. An email just wouldn't do!

The actor who played my father on *One Tree Hill*, John Doe, is one of the godfathers of punk music. He went on tour after leaving our show and would send me wonderful postcards from all over the country. They never depicted anything wildly interesting— always old motels and sightseeing spots from bygone eras fallen into ruin. It was as if he collected them for years knowing that eventually he would have the right recipient, and I felt so honored that he sent them to me.

Joy Lenz was another outstanding writing partner. Gifted with an aesthetic that is super feminine and nostalgic and whimsical, Joy creates full art pieces with her letters. She'll cut out flowers from magazines and snippets of poetry and decorate the paper before adding her loopy cursive handwriting. We worked together on *One Tree Hill* every day, and yet when there were emotional or truly thoughtful things that needed to be said, Joy would gift them to me in a letter to keep forever.

WHEN I GRADUATED FROM PARK VIEW HIGH SCHOOL, BRUCE Johnson and I began exchanging letters. His letters brought me close to home. He and Bobbie had been my Park View parents; they stepped in to help guide me through college applications, and Bobbie helped me get all my scholarships. And the Johnsons were ballast to my conservative, very Republican family. Back when I was seventeen, they were the most radical people I knew—Bruce had served in the military but turned into a bearded pacifist who wore bell-bottoms, while Bobbie had served in the Peace Corps in Zaire (now the Democratic Republic of the Congo) in 1976 during the Ebola outbreak. They were deeply politically engaged and presented a liberal flip side to the coin of my up-bringing. The Johnsons did not have biological children, but they had produced crops of teenagers in Sterling Park, Virginia, that absolutely belonged to them, period. Decades and decades of students turned into Johnson offspring, and I am proudly among them. Mr. Johnson called his chosen children "Hoocher"—don't ask me why—but it was his way of telling us we were loved.

Mr. Johnson was diagnosed with multiple sclerosis my junior year. His balance would betray him here and there, and a cane entered the picture. But even with the fear of the uncertain looming ahead of him, he leaned on his Episcopal faith and the wisdom and patience he'd learned through the study of antiquity. And then in 2003 he retired from Park View. But Mr. Johnson never retired from teaching. His Facebook feed was filled with quotes and stories from the great thinkers and Christian martyrs and poets. One post discussed Virgil and the *Divine Comedy*, Dante's tale of journeying through the underworld after the death of his beloved. Virgil has a profound influence on this piece of work, not only as Dante's favorite writer of all time, but also as his story's guide through hell, purgatory, and paradise.

Mr. J's letters were also littered with quotes and wisdom, anecdotes about his and Bobbie's cats Quintus and Marcus, and boundless gratitude for Bobbie taking care of him. As his mobility decreased, his frequency in writing increased. The letters he sent during my years in North Carolina were especially treasured because I was so desperately seeking guidance. The Johnsons were always good for that. In an environment that had become increasingly unstable for me, they represented unconditional love and support. That mail from Mr. Johnson—as from so many other people who have wandered in and out of my life—is a crystallized visit with the person who sent it.

In an antiques shop in Wilmington, I found a beautiful old metal box painted with pastoral landscapes. Those landscapes look very much like the vistas I have at the farm today, but back then they seemed like a fantasy land. Just like Hester, I positioned a bookshelf in the front entry of my house between the door and the stairs. This is where I displayed my own first editions and kept my sacred box of letters. When meaningful mail would arrive, that pretty box was where I would tuck it away, knowing I would have it forever to go back and reread. As I've gotten older, this has proven to be immeasurably valuable. I've lost a number of the people whose letters live in that box, and so their thoughts and their handwriting and the smudges from their coffee cups and the envelopes that they licked closed and the stamps that they picked out—all of those details are treasures to me, more valuable than I could possibly explain.

The Art of Letter Writing

A letter always seemed to me like immortality because
it is the mind alone without corporeal friend.

—Emily Dickinson

*L*et's be real: emails are going to be ugly no matter what you do. But a paper letter can be decorated and adorned not only on the note itself, but also on the intimate inside of the envelope and the very public exterior. Items can be added to the parcel to add a sense of mood—flower petals, magazine cutouts, recipe cards, patches, buttons, feathers, poems, small shells, restaurant matches, confetti. No, wait. Not confetti. Seriously, don't put confetti in with your letter unless you're sending it to an enemy.

I take envelope art pretty seriously. For my own wedding invitations, I knew that postage would be about one dollar. And so rather than invest in single stamps, I created a collage of stamps that had meaning for Jeffrey and me. A Washington

State stamp and a two-cent stamp commemorating an old Arbor Day that happened to fall on Jeff's birthday, April 22. A Wolf Trap Farm Park stamp, honoring the first professional stage I ever worked on as an actress. The Edna St. Vincent Millay stamp, commemorating my favorite poet. There was a Love stamp from the early 1980s that I totally remember from childhood. And an Outer Banks stamp commemorating the Lost Colony, as a reminder of that tiny strip of beach where we'd spent so much time as a family. The last stamp was a cheery little lemon, a nod to the night we met, cutting lemons and talking shit into the wee hours of the morning. It was a detail that probably didn't register with everyone. But for those who looked closely, it was a way to celebrate our life together without having to write a word.

So, how do you start writing letters?

Don't think about it too much. No one's gonna think you're a weirdo. I mean, maybe they *will* think you're a weirdo, but the reward outweighs the risk. Hopefully it just results in a return letter that is equally weird.

First, pick your favorite color. Go buy a couple of good pens in that color ink, or indulge in a full spectrum of inks. Gather a stack of paper that excites you, something that feels good beneath your fingers and beckons to be written on. Pick one corner to doodle in. And take ten minutes, once a week, to connect with someone in a slow, old-fashioned way.

An easy gateway is special occasion mail: a handmade birthday card, a condolence card, or mail around a time when someone you know is struggling with hardship, such as a death anniversary. There are Christmas cards, of course, or one could branch out to create summer solstice mail or commemorate Groundhog Day. But in my book, nothing beats an unexpected piece of impromptu mail because someone was thinking of you for no particular reason.

You don't have to confess your soul. Maybe you see something in a magazine you want to share, or you recently experienced something that reminded you of the person you're writing to. It's the check-in that counts. The actual contents are secondary.

Send people a memory they can hold in their hands. Or an idea or a joke or a compliment. If you're feeling stuck, take a walk and describe what you see. Write about a book you read, or something that made you laugh or cry, or feel something, anything at all. If a whole letter feels overwhelming, you could go the way of the postcard. Short and sweet, but still paper that arrives in a mailbox with your handwriting, a personal, inimitable touch. Letter writing is one of my favorite habits, and I feel so fortunate to have had pen pals who have had a deep impact on my life.

THE COVEN
YOU KEEP

I am a collector of powerful women.

Throughout my entire life, I have been drawn to groups of magnetic, complicated, bright creatures. Some of them are intimidating and loud, some quiet and cutting. Others are gentle and hold power through their softness. I'm stronger and smarter and more comfortable in my own skin for knowing them. They're my ride-or-dies, my army, my squad. You could also say they are my *coven*.

I didn't initially set out to create a coven. Thinking back on my group of girlfriends in high school, I never would have called us that. My initial image of the word came from studying *Macbeth*, with that coven of witches depicted as something sinister and dangerous. Little did I know that when I'd grown a bit older, the idea of a bunch of salty broads hanging out together and making mischief would sound more and more delicious.

My high school friends Ashley, Erica, Tory, and I would watch movies like *The Divine Secrets of the Ya-Ya Sisterhood*, *Now and Then*, and *Practical Magic* and imagine ourselves as a powerful group. But we were just playacting, weren't we?

We actually had a name for ourselves. It spawned one night while we were having a slumber party at Ashley's house and watching a beauty pageant to poke fun at it. It wasn't the first or last time we did this. Were we assholes? A hundred percent. But it was a wholesome all-American pastime for snarky fifteen-year-old girls in the 1990s.

One infamous contestant had a little trouble walking in her high heels and ended up looking like Sasquatch lurching across the stage. You know the iconic footage I'm talking about. Where the massive creature lumbers by, swinging his arms?

We loved it. We loved it so fucking much.

We dubbed that night Squatch-Fest and subsequently gave our ourselves the name "the Squatches." Bigfoot became our icon, and we would send each other greeting cards, T-shirts, socks, and other Squatch paraphernalia over the years.

Here we are in our early forties, and we still refer to ourselves as the Squatches. A Squatch-Fest is a getaway from husbands and children and work and all the responsibilities that turn our hair gray. It allows us to return to our fifteen-year-old selves. This coven is shared history and freedom and fun.

But the first time I actually was aware I was part of a coven was in my mid-twenties, working on *One Tree Hill*.

That was a hard time for me. I was lost. I couldn't figure out why I was still so adrift as a young adult, so I started paying attention to the women around me at work. I was particularly drawn to a woman named Mamacita. Now, that's not her real name. But she had a vibrant maternal personality and a honey-thick Southern drawl, so that's what everyone called her.

Mamacita was a hairdresser on *One Tree Hill*. But really, she was a balm for the toxic situation happening on set. She would lay hands at the base of my neck when she could tell I was particularly overwhelmed. She introduced me to women who talked about wild things like clearing chakras, and auras and spiritual guides. Mamacita wore white every day and looked like she was headed to a Southern baptism at any moment, with her skirts billowing and her thick, dark hair curled up into pillow-soft waves. (There was strong Elisabeth Chant energy coming from my sweet Mamacita.)

Do you ever meet someone who gives you warm fuzzies whenever you speak with them? Mamacita is warm and fuzzy personified.

I knew her to be an incredibly devout Christian. My Appalachian sweetheart loved Jesus more than anybody and would talk to you at length about faith and spirituality in a way that was never preachy, but inclusive and sincere. I liked her brand of Christianity. She would say things to me when I would get frustrated, like "if you're green you grow, but if you're ripe you rot." An evangelical soothsayer.

I'd also heard a couple of rumors about Mamacita being a bit of a witch. And that didn't make sense to me.

How could someone be a Christian and a witch?

Look, I was that little girl in Virginia who went to church regularly and hung out at youth group and dated boys in Christian rock bands and played Bible Jeopardy and was in Fellowship of Christian Athletes. I'd never heard anything about being a church girl and a mystic.

Well, it was time to dig into those Appalachian roots and learn about the generations of women that had come before me.

I will never forget one particular day for as long as I live. We were filming out on location, and our trailers were parked in a field surrounded by soft, feathery pine trees. The hair and makeup trailer was the epicenter of hive activity in our little base camp. And Mamacita happened to be working that day.

I went into the trailer with a pair of shorts on, lamenting that a wart on my knee was back.

It was so embarrassing! I'd had this wart off and on since I was in middle school, and it gave me a hell of a lot of insecurity. My childhood love, Larry Eppard, used to make fun of my knees, and so I went through every ritual to get rid of the damn thing.

I burned it off.

I shaved it off

I froze it off.

I carved it out.

I tried creams and lotions and potions, and not a damn thing worked.

It would go away for a minute and always come back. The scars accumulated. So here I was on a TV show where I was constantly in a skirt, and this wart had returned and I was pretty daggum mad about it. I sat in the makeup chair, getting my face painted, and Mamacita made her way over to examine it. She was somber. She took a good look at it. And she said in her thick accent, "Can I buy it off you?"

Now, I will tell you that sometimes her accent would be a little bit confusing. So, I thought I heard her say, "Can I *bite* it off you?"

And I burst out laughing! "Sure!" I said, thinking she was gonna lean down and bite it off my knee, or at least pretend to.

But instead, she put a penny in my palm, placed her hand over my wart, and then started muttering something I couldn't make out. She motioned with her hand like she was pinching the wart off my knee and then flung an imaginary thing away, repeating the action multiple times. Then she said, "Thank you so much," and she hightailed out of the trailer into those pine trees and appeared to be burying something.

I had never experienced anything like that before. And it was a display of theatrics that I loved. I didn't care if it worked; I just thought it was a cool little ritual. Mamacita came back in the trailer after a while and said, "Don't touch it. It will go away in just a few days and it won't be a problem anymore."

I have a healthy amount of skepticism, even though I do declare that I believe in everything. I wonder how much of medicine and magic is all placebo effect. But I smiled and nodded and I thanked her for not biting my wart off, but rather buying it for the price of a penny.

And then I went about my business.

I shit you not, that wart disappeared within a week! I thought for sure this thing would come back. Why wouldn't it? It had come back dozens of times before. But God as my witness, here I am fifteen years later and my knee is the best it's ever looked. Baby smooth! I don't question it. I don't doubt it. But I'm sure as hell grateful for it.

Once Mamacita had done her magic on me, it rang a bell. I had always heard stories of my grandmother being able to heal burns, but I couldn't wrap my head around *how* she could have done that. Was Mamacita the key to my Appalachian birthright?

"How'd you do it?" I finally worked up the nerve to ask.

Mama smiled and shook her head. "Can't tell ya, sister. My

daddy taught me, and you can only pass the knowledge man to woman, or woman to man."

Another bell rang! I remembered hearing that this was exactly how my grandmother's gift was passed along.

Well, I couldn't get enough of this, and like seems to attract like, so a third party entered the conversation. Wendybird was a makeup artist on our show. (I called her this because she reminded me of the wide-eyed, imaginative Wendy from *Peter Pan*.) She was quiet and intentional, the way artists often are. When she spoke, she meant every word she said, and she didn't participate in gossip or idle chatter. She was the kind of person who you could sit down with and talk about big ideas. And she was so calm that I found myself envious of her. I'm a hyper kid. Or at least I *was* a hyper kid. Now I'm a hyper old lady.

She'd been painting my face for the show off and on for years, but once she heard I was curious about witchery, a new door was opened. Wendy traveled to mystical places and read the kinds of books that I wanted to read. She always found time to challenge my beliefs and teach me new things, such as how to draw down the moon when it's full, or how to make meals with magical ingredients like pomegranate seeds. Wendy did facials in town when she wasn't working on our show. And I would go see her on my off days and listen to her tell stories about the visionaries and spiritualists in her circle.

Whereas Mamacita practiced old, multigenerational Appalachian magic, Wendybird was forward-looking and focused on enlightenment and the betterment of your soul. Being with them was a meditative experience.

(It's important to note here that I had known both of these

women for years. But it wasn't until I opened myself up and put out the energy of curiosity that we all started sharing ideas. Lesson learned. Open up if you wanna deepen your interactions!)

So, the three of us started palling around and hanging out at Mamacita's house, which had been lovingly dubbed "Serenity Now," in humorous reference to the 1997 Seinfeld episode.

Serenity Now consisted of her little arts and crafts bungalow, full of shabby-chic furniture and crystals and trinkets and pictures and an entire room of her vintage clothing. And then it expanded into the backyard, where she had a hot tub under a gazebo of flowering vines. I loved Serenity Now and I loved being with these women. Eventually we dubbed ourselves "The Secret Sisterhood of the Sylph."

A sylph is an air spirit, and we were all very committed to living our lives as fairies flitting around the flowers and other beautiful things, using our energy intentionally while drinking Chablis out of Mamacita's vintage goblets and reading from books that Wendybird had collected over the years.

They gave me this refuge, where I felt safe. The Secret Sisterhood of the Sylphs understood when I told them I had fallen in love with a man in the Land of Enchantment (New Mexico), and they hid me while I was pregnant with my son and I didn't want to be under the microscope of people who could have cast judgment.

We would invite all the other women from work into our group, creating a much larger coven. And I think those ladies would all play along for the novelty of it. But that true coven of my heart-sisters was Wendybird and Mamacita. They gave me permission to start reading the kinds of books that were banned when I was a younger woman. They gave me permission to explore in a way that was wholesome and spiritual and divine. They could also throw down crude jokes from time to time. They laughed heartily and told stories that made me want to be bold.

MOVING TO RHINEBECK IN 2010 PRESENTED ME WITH A COMpletely blank slate. Jeffrey and I didn't know anybody and my interactions were largely limited to grocery shopping and walking around town, until Gus turned three and I began taking him to preschool. The moms in the parking lot all seemed to know each other and despite what you might think, I still harbor those elementary school feelings of being the odd girl out.

There were two moms in particular to whom I felt drawn, and they were as different as night and day.

Sharagim Kemp is a supernova. From day one, she was the mom with the big smile and warm hugs who went out of her way to include people. I like watching people from afar before I start interacting with them, and what I witnessed was this wildly accomplished doctor—holding a toddler with one hand and carrying an infant with the other—listen to all these other parents with clear empathy as they described their maladies. I watched her help people and dispel the fear of illness, which is endless when you have snotty, rash-prone preschoolers all rolling around with each other. I remember laughing the first time she spoke to me. It was chaos at a parents' night, and everyone was jockeying for parking. An Iranian beauty who grew up in Southern California, she leaned in and muttered to me, "Where the fuck is the valet?"

"Dude. It's literally the only thing I miss about LA."

And that was that. We were friends. Our sons became joined at the hip, and Sharagim became the perfect yin to my yang. Where I'm perfectly content to hide on my farm, she throws hellacious parties on a regular basis. I'm the country mouse while she is the globe-trotting city mouse.

MY OTHER PRESCHOOL MOM-FRIEND IS TARA SHAFER. TARA IS MY cosmic twin. We share the same birthday of July first. We both are obsessed with Robby Benson's performance in the filmed stage version of *Our Town*. The first time I entered her house, I spied the entire series of Katie John books, an out-of-print collection from the early 1960s about a tomboy that I was *infatuated* with. "I've never met anyone else who knows about Katie John!" I said.

"We're the same person," Tara answered. And it's true. She first got my attention because she was the only other mother who parked at the far, far, *far* back of the parking lot. She didn't dress up, was aloof in a sexy, mysterious way, and was clearly a stellar mother. She had two older kids who would visit the preschool, and they were overwhelmingly kind and polite and smart. I was nervous the first time we struck up a conversation. I'd heard that she was consulting on a movie about stillbirth and fell into deep discussion with her in the grocery store. "There are so many talented women living here in the Hudson Valley," she'd said. "We all moved here for our kids, but we need to cultivate spaces for us to work. To contribute." Oh man, I wanted to be on her team.

YEARS LATER, TARA SENT ME A POEM. "READ THIS AT MY FUNERAL," she instructed.

It was "Ithaka" by C. P. Cavafy. I gasped. One particular stanza stood out.

Keep Ithaka always in your mind.
Arriving there is what you're destined for.
But don't hurry the journey at all.
Better if it lasts for years,
so you're old by the time you reach the island,
wealthy with all you've gained on the way,
not expecting Ithaka to make you rich.

"Tara! I grew up on Ithaca!" There was no way she could have known that. You are just naturally drawn to certain people.

Sharagim and Tara are still my constant advisors. Tara brings poetry to our circle, while Sharagim fixes us with evil-eye pendants and heaps of food that she infuses with love and magic.

I elaborate further in my book *The Rural Diaries*, but when I had my own miscarriage, these two new friends sprang into action. Sharagim doctored me with a firm and loving hand, helping heal my body so I could have another baby in the future. And Tara helped me understand my feelings and process the pain so that I could be present and alive for my family.

A new coven was formed.

These friendships, these sacred covens, keep me going when life feels overwhelming; they give me safety when the world seems to be falling apart. They remind me who I am at my core; they reflect it back to me.

AFTER A RECENT PARTY, SHARAGIM AND I HEADED TO MY HOUSE to enjoy the warm summer on my back deck. In the wee hours of the morning, we gossiped and giggled and were making perfect asses of ourselves, when we noticed that the sky seemed to have an unnatural symmetry.

Extraordinary bright lights lined up in a perfect row across the cosmic canvas. Sharagim, ever the practical one, pulled out her phone, downloaded an app, and aimed it toward the sky. Hot damn! The planets were visible to the naked eye and strung like glittering beads on a chain around the cosmos's neck. As our Earth tilted on its axis, they revealed themselves to us one by one.

Through the app, we saw the outermost planets of Neptune and Uranus. But we only needed the naked eye to witness the performance of Saturn and Jupiter. Mars was aggressive in its bright red show. Next, the hot-pink crescent moon of June came up from the horizon and looked like something from a Lisa Frank calendar. And Venus rose after that, with Mercury so close behind that they twinkled on top of each other in the distance.

It was a perfect planetary alignment. And they are not common. We looked it up: the next one won't happen until 2040, and the one after that won't occur until 2854! We had witnessed something extraordinary, and by total accident. We hadn't stayed up that late in forever. We're moms; normally we put the kids to bed and then pass out. But on this random night in June, when we decided to stay up until three o'clock in the morning discussing all the big and serious decisions we needed to be making, we got a cosmic show that felt like a spiritual reward. So, I link arms with my past and current covens. We make our own Planetary Parade.

Line up together and you'll be more beautiful, just like those planets.

Celestial Bodies

To give your magic a boost, try timing it with the phase of the moon. For things that won't wait, go with the day of the week that works best.

—Amy Blackthorn, *Blackthorn's Botanical Magic:
The Green Witch's Guide to Essential Oils for Spellcraft,
Ritual & Healing*

*Y*ou know the quote, "We are made of star-stuff." Carl Sagan wasn't kidding.

I've heard it mentioned in songs. *Thank you, Moby.* The early 2000s let us know, "no one can stop us now, 'Cause we are all made of stars."

I've heard it in poetry. Nikita Gill's "93 Percent Stardust" is a favorite.

I have heard it in love letters from shitty boyfriends.

And most recently, I've heard it expounded upon at a number of funerals.

There's a reason we cling to that imagery. Because it's true! There has always been an intersection between science and witchiness. This idea of humans being made from the cosmos could have been heresy back in the day. How dare a person suggest that we spawned from anything other than a literal interpretation of the Bible! Burn the witch!

However, the number of atoms in the universe is finite. Matter is finite. And the building blocks of life—carbon, hydrogen, nitrogen, oxygen, phosphorus, and sulfur—are products of stars turning to supernovas over billions of years!

So, it makes all the sense in the world that we are drawn to the sky. Whether looking to the stars to help us make sense of who we are or to the planets themselves, we are celestial bodies. And while we're born under a certain zodiac sign (I love that the older we get, the more those signs actually seem pretty spot on. I am a Cancer all ding-dong day!), the solar system really lends itself to being a matter of preference. Let's take a look at each of the planets and see what speaks to you.

MOON: Okay, this first one isn't a planet, but I have to start here because I have been smitten with the moon since childhood. If you follow me on social media, this is not a surprise. I post pictures with my girlfriend the moon shining her big, beautiful face on me all the time. I love reveling in her evolution from flirty little crescent to bold and suggestive fullness. My waxing girl encourages me to start new things and take risks and begin, begin, begin! And my waning sweetheart lets me know it's okay to release, to clean out those closets, to say no to things.

The tidal push and pull within me has been synced with the moon forever and as women, we are absolutely connected: our periods ebb and flow with the moon. In pregnancy, our labors are affected by her fullness. We know how much the moon affects the push and pull of the ocean waves and the tides of the bay. And understanding that we as humans are made of between 50 to 60 percent water, it seems a matter of scientific fact that the moon is our orchestra leader.

I wear moonstone to remind myself to practice calmness. I regard the moon as a reminder of my own evolution, ever changing, beautiful in each phase. The universe gives us hints as to how we should behave. And so, we just have to listen.

JUPITER: When I posed this question to my sisters on the *Drama Queens* podcast—"What is your favorite planet?"— Sophia made me laugh so hard because she is *hot* for Jupiter. Now, this makes a world of sense to me. As someone who loves her deeply, she is 100 percent a Jupiter person.

She says it's because she likes the desert color palette. But I know it's because my girl is a big, gigantic swirl of ideas and activism and leadership and generosity. Jupiter has an inner core about the size of Earth, but it is surrounded by a massive amount of hydrogen and helium like the sun, making it the biggest planet in our system. It has more than eighty moons. It's magnetic the same way Sophia is, and is the fastest rotating planet. Spot fucking on.

If you're wanting to expand your own worldview or manifest abundance in your life, work with the color yellow and schedule big decisions on Thursdays.

EARTH: Meanwhile, Joy asserts that her favorite planet is none other than Earth. This is a *perfect* answer. Earth, with its supportive atmosphere, is home to a biodiversity that is unparalleled. We've found evidence of previous life forms in other parts of the solar system, but on Earth, life is abundant, as it is with Joy. She is a warm and nurturing person, and she makes things come alive! Music. Fashion. Home improvement projects. Scripts. Global adventuring. Cocktails. She is as lush and varied as Mother Earth, and much like our home planet— the only one with tectonic plates in our system—Joy is the kind of woman who can move mountains.

MARS: Covered in vivid red dust due to an abundance of iron, it's a planet for the toughest among us. Named for the Roman god of war, Mars is the planet for those who do not shy away from confrontation and can handle a hellacious dust storm or two.

If you're a fan of Mars, give Ray Bradbury's *Martian Chronicles* a whirl. It portrays a frontier that is romantic in its mysteries. Did ancient aliens build pyramids on the planet's surface, and are there underground rivers or living organisms? Will we build ecosystems under great bubbles on the surface of that planet and be living there within a generation? Mars people don't hesitate to explore bold ideas.

Put your competitive Mars energy to work on the planet's aligned day—Tuesday. Wear red and raise hell!

VENUS: Fans of Venus are sensual and understand the beauty of small things, small gestures, small moments. A sideways glance. A hand that lingers for a moment too long. She is obviously the hottest planet in our system and she burns very, very bright in our night sky. If you catch her on the right night, it's clear that she is a planet of pleasure. Also worth noting, Venus spins in the opposite direction of most of the planets. If you love her, go on with your sexy little rebellion!

Venus's day of the week is Friday, so practice a little love magic with a symbol of the Love goddess—fresh flowers.

MERCURY: Mercury is the planet closest to the sun but has extreme highs and lows in temperatures. It also has a massive molten iron core, with a thin shell. So, if you are one of my temperamental friends with a thin skin? Boy, have I got the planet for you! Named for the Roman god Mercury—better known as Hermes in Greek mythology—this is the messenger planet, and the character in charge of helping travelers along their way. This makes sense, given that Mercury is the fastest orbiting planet. It's a fearless planet, as it is unintimidated by the sun, much like Mercury/Hermes was unintimidated to bring souls down to the afterlife. Brave and grumpy. I know a *bunch* of Mercury people. These folks should do their most important messaging on the planet's affiliated day—Wednesday.

SATURN: With its showy rings, this is an interesting planet for people to favor. It's for my friends who appreciate standing out in the crowd and being different. They know how to navigate with a great deal swirling around them. I don't want to say they're self-involved. However, it's worth noting that while Saturn spins super fucking fast on its own axis, it takes its sweet time rotating around the sun. Twenty-nine Earth years, to be exact. And as if that wasn't enough, it rains literal *diamonds* on Saturn. How could the Romans have known this when they named the planet after the god of wealth and the harvest? So, if you are fancy AF and don't care who knows, you are a Saturn baby. This planet is affiliated with binding or restricting, maybe because of those wild rings. This is the planet to invoke when you want to shush the judgment or the haters.

URANUS: I remember having to do planet reports in third grade. Everybody wanted Venus or Mars. As the girl with huge glasses and buck teeth and wild hair, naturally my teacher did me the great favor of assigning me Uranus. So of course when I had to present my speech about my planet, it was a mortifying exercise in talking over butt jokes. I couldn't tell you anything about Uranus (insert dirty joke here) because I wasn't drawn to that planet. I was a moon girl.

Poor Uranus failed to capture my attention in third grade, but I'm sure there is a select percentage of people out there who think it's a perfectly cool planet. It's pretty far from the sun, making it more of a mystery than some of these other guys. And it's for sure the coldest. That icy atmosphere gives it a very chill aqua color and its own gorgeous rings. If Saturn is too much of a braggart for your taste, try sleepy Uranus. It's the low-key grandpa planet. But he wasn't always so calm.

According to Greek myth, Uranus (Father Sky) had babies with Mother Earth, resulting in the Titans. He was kind of an overbearing husband and father. As a result, he got castrated by one of his kids and his balls fell into the ocean to create Aphrodite. So . . . take that metaphor and do whatever you want with it. Ha! Uranus is definitely a counterculture planet to lean into, so wear blue as you invoke it to support radical ideas and rebellion.

NEPTUNE: We've only known about this planet for a little under two hundred years. Neptune has wind speeds over 2,000 miles per hour. It also holds a ton of water, and that all tracks because it's named after the god of the sea, the Roman equivalent to the Greek Poseidon. Those who identify with Neptune are overflowing with emotions, creativity, spirituality, and all the rest of the tear-inducing subjects. Neptune fans are deep-feeling creatures, and perhaps a bit distant. I feel like every moody poet from my sordid youth spent in coffee shops had a Neptune streak. It can be incredibly attractive.

Try your hand at manifesting through watercolor painting if you are a sensitive Neptune fan.

PLUTO: And then there's that sweet little dumplin' who keeps getting its planet status taken away and returned and taken away and returned. Pluto is for my friends who love an underdog, much like Pluto the god, who loved his kingdom in the underworld. I will always view Pluto as a planet, damn all the scientists! I will always respect its tenacity to keep floating there in the sky, hangin' with the rest of the big kids in the solar system. Even if it's the last one picked for the kickball team. If you are a fan of Pluto, you're more than likely an empath, wanting everyone to feel included.

Go celebrate what is under the surface by making your manifestations and burying them.

SYNCHRONICITIES

I'm gonna let you in on a little secret.

This entire book is a synchronicity.

It was the summer of 2021. My friends Sophia Bush and Joy Lenz and I had recently launched a rewatch podcast of the show we did together when we were brand-new little animals, *One Tree Hill*. This joint project had been years in the making. Our time together on that particular job had been fraught with shitty leadership and toxic boy bosses. And while we are all women who know how to make a mean glass of lemonade from the sour citrus of life, analyzing those years was going to be an emotional experience. I'd be lying if I said I was 100 percent sure revisiting that time in a podcast was a good move. Ultimately, I just wanted a do-over with my sweet friends.

After private talks, we realized that we all wanted to take ownership of the experiences that were good, while calling out the horrendous stuff. But after watching the pilot episode with the girls, I was a wreck. We had to take a good, long moment before taping the podcast so I could pull myself together. I forgot just how young I was way back when. I forgot what a determined little idealist I was. Same goes for my sisters. We were kids.

While I simultaneously continued taping podcasts and working on this book, the *Drama Queens* podcast premiere crept ever closer. I was a ball of nerves. And then, as it does when you let the universe surprise you, I got a package in the mail.

Y'all know how I feel about mail.

A year before, I had sent a general inquiry to Scott Power, an art dealer in North Carolina:

"I'm curious about the price of your Claude Howell *Beach Cottage* painting. Any pieces by him or Elisabeth Chant or Hester Donnelly are of particular interest to me. Thank you so much."

The art dealer did in fact have a couple of Claude Howells and sent me this reply:

"Thanks for contacting me about works on my site. I actually have three works by Claude Howell for sale. I've included pictures and information on all three. As I'm sure you're aware, Elisabeth Chant's works are extremely hard to come by and highly prized, but I don't have anything by her. I have had several Hester Donnelly pieces of Wilmington scenes but right now I don't have anything by her either. I'll certainly keep my eyes peeled."

Okay, we were getting somewhere. The Howells were great, but what I was really after was a Hester Donnelly piece. I wrote back:

"So grateful for your help. I owned Hester Donnelly's house for years and got to know some of the older crowd she used to run with in Wilmington. The house was quite haunted. Fun to imagine the artsy get-togethers in that parlor."

Many months later, in April 2021, he sent a message.

"I didn't know if you still had an interest in Hester Donnelly's work, but I recently acquired the one that I've attached a photo of. If you have any interest, just let me know. Thanks."

Yes! Of course I wanted the painting! I sent a response immediately.

But the package wouldn't arrive right away. I was traveling with the kids from Georgia, where Jeff was filming, back up to the farm for the summer, so I wasn't in any rush. Scott could mail it whenever he got a minute. The small business hustle is no joke, and I never want to be one of those customers that stamp their foot like Veruca Salt and demand, "I want it NOW!"

And so, I waited for Hester to visit me again.

Wouldn't you know, Hester's painting—my memento of my ghostly fairy godmother—arrived on the exact day that the *Drama Queens'* trip-down-memory-lane podcast premiered: June 21, 2021.

As I opened the package, I laughed. It made perfect sense to me that Hester's painting would show up the exact day of our podcast launch. I'd been nervous about my place in the world and revisiting a complicated chapter. But the same way Hester helped me make friends as a young adult, she showed up just in time to remind me that creating community is about taking risks and putting yourself out there. And that being "gruff and wonderful" is a helluva way to become a part of history.

I hung the watercolor painting of boats in the Cape Fear River above my desk, where I could see it while I worked.

I was invigorated. I set out to work on the Hester chapters of this book, but started to second-guess myself. It had been so many years since I lived in the Nun Street house. *Was I remembering everything correctly?*

But then in another bout of synchronicity, I got a very strange butt dial late at night. My ringer had been off, and so I'd slept through the call. But I woke up in the morning to discover Rabbi George's name on my caller ID.

I hadn't heard from him in well over a decade! I was amazed he still had my number. The last time we'd seen each other, Gus was just learning to walk. Now my boy was growing a mustache.

It was an accidental dial, and when I texted him the next morning so excited to reconnect, Rabbi George was apologetic. I wrote him back: *It really was beautiful timing to get your text and I'll take it as a sign from the universe to reconnect. You are very missed! If you were open to it, I'd love to catch up and pick your brain about Hester and Nun Street.* That sweet man then talked to me for hours, confirming what I already knew and adding much more information to the Legend of Hester.

Summer turned into fall, and there was tragedy and loss and the practicalities of balancing motherhood with career. As I moved through grief, writing this book took on a deeper importance. I am not ashamed to admit that in trying to write about legacy and passion for living, I was absolutely stuck.

I needed help. We had lost an alarming number of loved ones in rapid succession, and the constant barrage of death had left me numb. I knew what I wanted to create for my own children, and what I wanted to encourage others to create for themselves. But I needed to be jolted from my dark place. And just like that, Tara appeared with the answer.

Wethersfield.

Built by her grandfather Chauncey Stillman, Wethersfield is a grand Golden Age estate built not terribly far from my farm in the middle of nowhere, where Tara works as the executive director of the board. Her entire goal with the property is to make it a safe haven for young people practicing classical arts. Ballerinas dance among the topiaries. Painters capture dreamy sunsets and the unparalleled vistas of the estate. Writers give lectures in front of the statuary. It's a magical spot, and a place where we have let our kids daydream and explore. But we all know the arts are in peril, and so she asked for my help in raising awareness of the property and the programming.

Did I have the time? Nope. My house was under construction, my kids were being homeschooled, my husband was away filming in Georgia, that podcast with my *OTH* sisters had blown up, and I felt the responsibility of producing my first unscripted series, *It Couldn't Happen Here*, covering horrible injustices in rural communities like my own. And the darkness I was wading through during that show contributed even more to my serious writer's block. What was the point in writing about magic when you couldn't see your way out of sorrow? (In fact, that's *exactly* why we write our magic down! To remind ourselves of what is light and good and powerful when the going gets tough!)

Needless to say, I was messy. This seems to be a running theme with *any* project I work on.

Messy is honest! But all this left me feeling so miserable, I knew the only way to get out of my funk was to focus on other people. Plus, Tara is a magical person to be with. Helping her would be good for my head.

She sent over a bunch of information on the property: maps, analysis of the statues in the garden, letters from her grandfather, websites to give historical context. It was clear that Mr. Stillman drew a huge amount of inspiration from ancient Greek mythology, and he had filled the entire estate with massive statues that dotted the landscape not only in the formal gardens near the house, but throughout the depths of the wooded acreage as well.

It looked as though Medusa had wandered through the estate, turning folks to stone. I appreciated that; I'm someone who has loved the Gorgon goddess since childhood. The awful kids in elementary school would call me Medusa to mock my unruly hair. Turns out it didn't hurt my feelings, just gave me a goddess to look up to! I wore a Medusa pendant all through *One Tree Hill*, and not knowing that, during the first emotional season of my Sundance docuseries, Sharagim gave me a Medusa bracelet to keep me safe.

Since there were Greek and Roman gods involved at Wethersfield, I knew that if anyone could walk me through the intricacies of antiquity, it was Mr. Johnson.

There was a rumor that this elaborate garden at Wethersfield was in fact a Dante Garden, based on Dante's *Divine Comedy*, the tale of Dante being guided through the nine circles of Hell and through Purgatory before he could ascend into Paradise:

> In the middle of the journey of our life,
> I came to myself, in a dark wood, where the direct
> way was lost.

Starting in the forest and moving up through the hilltop that overlooked 360-degree views of the Hudson Valley, the gardens were divided into three distinct sections. The Inferno section was laid out through the depths of the forest with large, ominous gates subtly warning you to beware. The Purgatory garden began as the land ascended and dense trees gave way to intentionally planted hedges of laurel. And then there was Paradisio, the most meticulous of Italian formal gardens, atop the hill of Wethersfield. It was gonna be a *ton* of work, and I was already spread thin with my other jobs. But I could not wait to talk to Mr. Johnson about this new endeavor. He was the king of this subject matter! He had started treatment for a manageable form of cancer, and so the kids and I sent check-in videos of autumn activities on the farm and visits with Santa.

As I compiled the chapters of this book from various journals I'd kept over the years, the theme of mythology kept resurfacing. With this new puzzle piece of Wethersfield in the mix, I could start to see how my story—and all of our stories—could be laid out.

We are all Odysseus, longing for the home of our heart. We fight battles and monsters in our attempts to return to Ithaca.

We are all Dante, wandering through the despair of the Inferno in hopes of emerging into Paradise. We are all creating our own personal mythologies!

This new lens gave me back the creative spark I'd been missing, and I kicked off New Year's Day by finally writing again. On January 2, 2022, I finished the chapters in this book on Ithaca and Rebellion. I knew the idea of home would be the cornerstone of this book, because it is the cornerstone of magic. It is our personal church. It is where we practice our rituals and the truest magic, love. Mr. and Mrs. Johnson were the first people I visited whenever I made my way home after years of being away. I was excited to share all the ideas bouncing around in my head and hear the Latin expert's feedback.

The next icy morning, I dropped Gus off at school and ran to the CVS in town to grab a few things. I'd kept my ringer on, which I never do. And when it started buzzing, I just assumed it was Gus's school.

It wasn't.

Devastated to let you know Bruce died in his sleep. Mrs. Johnson had sent the text. I dropped what I'd gathered and ran to my car.

It doesn't matter how prepared you think you are, or how practiced you are with loss. It's still a sucker punch that waits until you are unprepared for the impact. I called Mrs. Johnson and sobbed. Drove home. Sobbed to my husband. And then I made the decision to get in the car and drive to Virginia. There was a snowstorm that day and Mrs. Johnson was worried about me driving down. But somehow, over the course of that seven-hour drive, I missed all the terrible weather, and I pulled into her driveway right around dinnertime. I needed that long drive to gather my thoughts, and cry, and focus on being a calm presence for this woman who meant so much to me. But I couldn't help being angry that the person I was most excited to share this Wethersfield project with was gone. We were going to have an adventure. All the letters, all the Latin quotes, all the references to the Romans and ancient gods . . . it was cruel timing.

Mrs. J and I hugged and put on brave faces and fell apart and pulled it together. She was wearing the cross necklace made from an ancient Roman coin I'd given Mr. Johnson for his birthday a couple of years before. We drank bourbon with her nieces and looked at pictures. And I sat at her feet as she told us stories of their time together teaching at Park View, starting in the late seventies. They'd lived only two or three blocks over from my house on Ithaca. The love for this home—one we could never return to—was a shared experience.

At some point that night, I went to use the bathroom in the front hallway. It was right next to Mr. Johnson's office, the place where he'd write his notes and correspond with his army of former students. There was a picture of us on his desk taken my senior year. I always loved that picture because I was really smiling in it. (I can always tell whether I'm faking it or smiling for real in old pictures, and Mr. Johnson was so gruff and no-bullshit, I loved his company. Real smiles all around.) But then I caught my breath. Behind the photo, on one of his packed bookshelves, was a bright red book with enormous letters on the cover: INFERNO.

Of course. He was still gently guiding me.

I was on my way back to Ithaca. Seeing Mr. Johnson's copy of *Inferno* in his office, the night of his passing felt like an instruction. Go into the dark wood . . .

Exactly a month later, my Squatch coven sister Erica called our gang out to Portland, Oregon, for her fortieth birthday. I'd never been out there, so Ashley, Tory, and I left our various spawn and made the cross-country trek for a thirty-six-hour party. Everywhere we went, there was a reference to Medusa. Paintings in shops. Snakes in jars. Medusa figurines in the toy shop. We had to meet some of Erica's local friends, so we started walking back to her house.

What should we find around the corner? Medusa. Painted on a wall.

Have you ever heard of synchronicity?

"The simultaneous occurrence of events that appear significantly related but have no discernable casual connection."

Basically, it's a big cosmic sign from the universe that things are lining up. Stay on the path!

Perhaps you've noticed that when you say a person's name, that person suddenly appears out of nowhere. This is a very real problem I have, so I'm careful whom I talk shit about when I hang out with my girlfriends from high school.

Maybe more common is seeing certain numbers over and over.

I'm one of those 11:11 creatures. I know folks who see 222 or 333, or other repeated numbers. I'm no expert on numerology or angel numbers, but I do know that in my own life, I pay very close attention to whom I am talking to or what I am doing in those moments where numbers are synchronizing for me. It's no big deal when it happens once or twice. But during certain phases of my life, this happens damn near every day. I'll take the hint! Much the same way dreams work, waking up to the symbolism in your life is a good practice to deepen your witchy abilities.

Naturally, my high school girlfriends had asked about the Johnsons and knew all about Ithaca. And I had told them enough about the Wethersfield project that all of us had a heightened awareness. My senses were tingling in Portland as we kept running into Medusa around every corner. *Synchronicity.*

We went out to lunch and had margaritas on the back patio of the restaurant, and it was good to be with my lifelong sisters and feel light for a moment. When Tory and I went inside to grab another round, we passed a group with an old, handsome German shepherd.

"Hi, buddy!" I said. "What a chill guy." I asked his owner, "Can I pet him?"

"Yeah, of course," his owner said. "This is his last big weekend, so we are soaking up all the pets."

"Oh no!" I could see how tired this sweet boy was, and I recognized the things that we had done with our own dog, Bisou, when her time was up. There was a burger for him. Ice cream. All the treats that puppies love. And he was being showered with attention. He leaned into my pets, and my friends and I took the time to commune with these strangers who were grieving with such grace. "What's his name?" Tory finally asked.

"Poseidon."

Our necks snapped to look at each other. The same Poseidon who thrust himself on virtuous Medusa in the temple of Athena while she was still gorgeous, causing the Goddess of War to curse the maiden with a headful of venomous snakes?? Huh. How 'bout that?

That night, Erica booked appointments for the four of us to get tattoos together. I had no idea what to get; I was just happy to be with my friends and was pretty much game for anything. The tattoo artists didn't really have any flash that was my style, or so I thought. "Dude," Erica said, grabbing the artist's binder. "Look at the cover." Snakes connected by their tails twisted and hissed. Their bodies were set up to frame any word or phrase you fancied. "Put Ithaca in there."

And so, I did.

Armed with the home of my heart on my hip, I was ready to head out of the dark wood, taking the ghosts and losses and lessons with me.

Write Your Own Eulogy

When people ask me where I get my ideas, I laugh.
How strange—we're so busy looking out, to find ways
and means, we forget to look in.

—Ray Bradbury

We eulogize the things we love when they are no longer
with us. It's how we show our reverence. Most commonly,
we eulogize loved ones, standing before crowds and recounting
their memorable qualities, or heartwarming stories of how they
walked among us. We eulogize people we've never met, gathering in the great funeral parlors of social media to mourn the loss
of beloved icons like Olivia Newton-John or Ronnie Spector or
literally any of the Golden Girls. It's how we memorialize restaurants that have gone out of business or shops on Main Street that
have been shuttered, cancelled TV shows and bands that have
broken up. We lift up the good in order to soothe the bad. *I loved
this*, we say. *I am changed because of it.*

But we don't do it for ourselves. We just trust that someone we love will handle that bit of paperwork for us. What are we thinking? We're missing out on all the fun! I realize how morbid that sounds, but writing your own eulogy isn't about anticipating your demise, it is about celebrating your life and setting your intentions for how to live. I want to be aware of what I'm living and creating in the moment. And I want to have a sense of honor—and humor—about it.

In chapter 1, I confided that I wanted to leave my kids with behaviors, traditions, funny habits, and a sense of curiosity that outweigh any material inheritance—and I work damn hard at that. But there are so many things they don't know about me, so many things they haven't seen and never will. That's probably true for you, too.

How many people in your life could rattle off your many, many passions, beliefs, loves, adventures, and salacious secrets?

Recently, I saw an article about a grandmother who had mini Ouija boards passed out at her funeral, with a note that said "Keep in Touch." Believe me when I tell you that I felt this note in my bones! The greatest gift we can give our loved ones in the wake of loss is laughter. So, darlings, that is why we are taking control of our own eulogies.

Open up your grimoire and start keeping a list of the things you'd want acknowledged at the end of your days. The plain fact of the matter is that if you're a parent, your obituary will say that you were a doting parent. Or if you are a spouse, or an employee of some company, it will say that you were a devoted partner/a hard worker. Yeah, yeah, yeah. That's all about who we are to other people. This list is about who you are to yourself!

What have you done in your life that has been a surprise?

What has been terrifying but empowering?

What kind of juicy gossip have you kept all to yourself? If you want a grand finale, better leave 'em with all the eyebrow-raising stories you got.

And while this exercise may focus on the finality of death, of all the tricks up my sleeve, this list has been the tool I turn to the most to keep me alive. There have been dark nights of the soul when failure and confusion have laid me low. And this list? This is my reminder that I'm fiercely alive. This is my reminder that there are surprises around every bend. This is my reminder that I'm not some soft and squishy old lady. I am a mischievous, daring tornado of a woman. And I made a beautiful mess during my time here.

Now, I'm not gonna give you my *whole* list. But just to give you some food for thought as you consider yours, here are some random entries, in no particular order.

1. Covered the 2002 Winter Olympics, went down the bobsled with the US team, learned to curl from the Russian women's team (put a dent in the ice so the entire arena had to be redone the night before competition. Whoops.)

2. Learned to two-step from a member of the Choctaw Nation at a honky-tonk in Texas.

3. USO tours, kissing dozens of soldiers as they deployed, sending pregnancy and baby announcement videos with wives and girlfriends, and doing physical fitness tests with marines.

4. Natural childbirth . . . twice.

5. Cooked for Martha Stewart.
6. Recorded a song in Nashville for my first movie.
7. Hosted NYE live shows in Times Square for five years.
8. Spent my birthday camping on an uninhabited island.
9. Ghost tours: New Orleans, Wilmington, Charleston, Paris, London, Salem, Kingston.
10. Helped people make masks in the pandemic.
11. Took shots for the first time in Canter's Deli's Kibitz Room.
12. Waited up to see the circus elephants march through the Midtown Tunnel to Madison Square Garden at 2 a.m.
13. Marched in the Greenwich Village Halloween parade.
14. Went to Loretta Lynn's ranch Hurricane Mills to see her perform with her family.
15. Went onstage at the Moulin Rouge and danced in a strange Parisian club where someone placed a large snake around my neck.

One of the most powerful elements to a successful grimoire is the act of remembering! We write down the knowledge we collect from others so that we may remember. But don't forget to remember yourself!

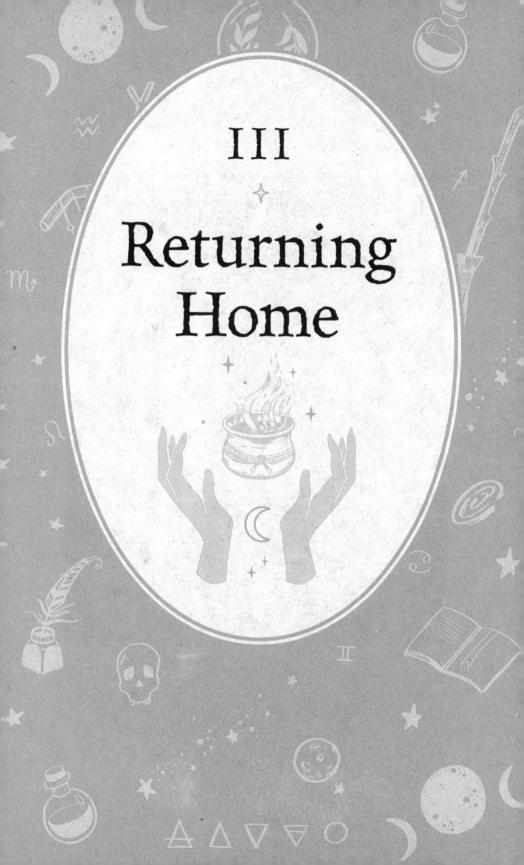

III

✦

Returning Home

LOOK TO
ANTIQUITY

hat is it about mythology that makes it universal and applicable to our lives, even if we don't practice ancient religions? Toddlers adore *D'Aulaires' Book of Greek Myths*. I love that the Percy Jackson series opened up the lessons of the Greek gods to a whole new generation of school kids. The soap opera qualities of love affairs on Mount Olympus seem particularly applicable during young adulthood. And even now as I get older, there are certain stories that personally ring true. After seeing an early performance of *Hadestown* on Broadway, I dug into the mythology surrounding Persephone and Hades. There are a number of different ways to interpret ancient narratives, and when I was a kid, I'd heard that Hades—God of the Underworld—kidnapped Persephone from her mother, Demeter, and made her his bride. She was eventually set free when Hermes demanded she be returned to the land of the living. But Hades sent Persephone a pomegranate and she ate the seeds, not knowing that they would bind her to the Underworld forever. (Or *did* she know?) An agreement was made: part of the year, Persephone would belong to the living, resulting in spring and summer; the remaining months were dedicated to living with her husband, giving us mortals fall and winter. But there are more than a few scholars who think Persephone knew exactly what she was doing and had to pretend she wanted to remain virtuous to her family, while she was actually enthralled by her mysterious and slightly dangerous god of a husband. It's worth noting that during the course of their marriage, heroes and visitors to the Underworld often encountered Queen Persephone. She was a trusted teammate to her husband, and he listened to her time and again. It's one of the few Greek god marriages that seem functional.

So, as I look at my own life, and examine my husband with his booming voice and dark nature, I get the Hades thing! Would a modern-day Hades have strong Negan energy? The idea of only seeing your spouse half the year doesn't seem so outlandish to me as an adult. Jeff has been on the road for work since we met, and it just makes the hellos and goodbyes more passionate. I liked that this was a marriage of two independent, strong personalities.

But the real intention of the Hades and Persephone story was to show the importance of duality, the magic of opposites. You cannot have the growth of spring without the decay and renourishing of the soil in winter. You cannot have the brutal truth of the Underworld without the sunshine and promise of future days in the garden. You need both masculine and feminine energies when making tough decisions. These are sentiments echoed throughout various world religions. It's just that the Greeks knew how to make it a really juicy story! Traces of those stories are sprinkled everywhere—from tattoo parlors in Portland, Oregon, to fountains in European towns, and even in the hidden dells of the Hudson Valley.

Tara and I had been friends for a number of years before she revealed Wethersfield to me. "I want to invite you over to my grandfather's house," she'd said years before she asked me for help publicizing the estate. She was nostalgic for summers spent there with her siblings, climbing trees and wandering through the forest. I envisioned a farmhouse, with a deep front porch. Something cozy and historic. A grandpa in flannel shirts, maybe smoking a pipe.

I was dead wrong.

Gus hopped into the car and I plugged the address into my phone and found myself rolling across the hills of horse country. You could tell by the well-appointed stone walls that curled along the countryside that these were the gentleman farms of the supremely wealthy. We were driving along the dusty path of a dirt road, and then the world shifted and we were enveloped in a tunnel of weeping willows dancing on the breeze. *Magic was afoot.* The willows pulled back to reveal massive brick estate walls, tall black iron gates, and stately bronze peacock statues perched on either pillar. On a hill stood a glamorous six-columned open-air temple overlooking the Catskill Mountain range. Gus and I crunched across a gravel lot that was more appropriate for a state park or a museum and entered into a garden, extravagant and formal in nature. It was a slice of seventeenth-century Italy, hidden perfectly in the rural obscurity of Amenia, New York.

"Tara! What the hell is this?"

She'd met us in the garden, knowing there was no way I'd be

able to find my way through the Alice-in-Wonderland hedges that grew out like acres of rooms from the exterior of the Georgian brick house. She was bashful. I knew my sensitive friend well enough to understand that this was someplace deeply emotional for her, and that sharing it with me was a signal of trust and love.

It may not have been my idea of a "grandpa house," but it was very much her grandpa's house, and he just happened to be Chauncey Stillman, heir to the Citibank fortune. Their family had been involved in the architecture of our nation, as Chauncey's wife, Theodora, was a descendant of John Jay. Frankly, the names and wealth and connections of the Gilded Age all sounded like something from an F. Scott Fitzgerald novel to me. As a kid, I didn't know this kind of extravagance existed. It was the opposite of the moment you find out Santa isn't real. This was the stuff of the fairy tales I'd read as a child—the mansion, the grounds, the family lore.

But Tara told stories of being dropped off here as a kid, of reading books by the reflecting pool, of carriage rides through the deep forest with her grandfather at the reins. Throughout the woods, enormous statues of Greek and Roman gods dotted the landscape. It was Narnia! Tara showed us her childhood hideaways, each bedroom of the estate unique and whimsical. Hanging the entire length of the circular staircase that was the centerpiece of the mansion was a needlepoint tapestry of a peacock, the family symbol, which Mr. Stillman had stitched himself. The famed fresco painter Pietro Annigoni found inspiration and refuge at the estate, painting large murals all over the home's gloriette, including the likenesses of Mr. Stillman and other members of the Wethersfield circle. There were secrets here. It was a space ripe with art and beauty, but also a melancholy I couldn't quite put my finger on.

WE WOULD GATHER THE KIDS IN THE GARDEN DURING THE following years, never really digging into its depths. And then when the pandemic hit and we all began homeschoooling, the garden at Wethersfield became a sanctuary. A new director of horticulture, Toshi Yano, had been hired in 2018 and brought with him an air of curiosity and restoration. (It's a fun sidenote that Toshi was a bassist in multiple hardcore bands of the 1990s and early 2000s, before touring with Franz Ferdinand for a stint. Rock 'n' roll gardener? Sign me up.) After a couple of seasons with the garden, he'd begun putting together the puzzle of Wethersfield. So, in 2020, after the great lockdown, Tara began sharing the bread crumbs that they had uncovered along those paths of the forest and formal gardens.

Toshi had gained an intimate understanding of the property and its physical qualities, where the land rose and fell. Where sunlight was abundant and where shadows grew long. He knew the colors and shapes each season of foliage displayed, and he understood that there were long forgotten enclaves that required patience and a keen eye to restore. During Mr. Stillman's life, the trails through the woods had been intentionally landscaped, but they had given themselves back over to Mother Nature in the last few decades. Toshi started the hard work of going back to maps and plans and designs from the late 1940s through Mr. Stillman's death in 1989. And as he compared the paperwork and the physical property, that Greek statuary could no longer be seen as random artwork. There was a story! A message!

Tara was working as executive director of Wethersfield Garden & Estate. It was a job title that sounded very serious to me, her very-lacking-in-blue-blood best friend. But in this position, she had begun using the property as a sanctuary for young artists. In the first winter of the pandemic, she opened the estate to BalletCollective, facilitating the only professional production of *The Nutcracker* in the entire country that holiday season. The formal living spaces of the home became the sets for the production, and a fresh blanket of snow frosted the gardens, where the Sugar Plum Fairy swirled and twirled.

Next, Tara shifted her focus to painting, and in came the young, talented artists of the Grand Central Atelier. Recreating the romanticism of the Hudson River School of painting, Tara let the artists live in Wethersfield and paint the astounding 360-degree views of the Catskill and Berkshire mountains. There was new life on the property after decades of quiet. And with each new visitor, Tara was forced to give a brief summary of the property's history. It wasn't easy; there was a lot of sadness in her grandfather's life, but also a lot of beauty and service and good.

The magic of storytelling is that each time we tell our story, it gets easier, we share more, and ideas begin to crystallize as we say them out loud. After years of knowing each other and the kind of friendship that sees you through all manner of shitstorm, Tara shared her family history with me.

As I mentioned before, Tara came to me at the exact moment I needed inspiration. "I need help raising awareness for the arts programming," she'd said. Well, awareness was my specialty! The success of the *Drama Queens* podcast with my *One Tree Hill* coven had been huge. It was a medium I liked very much, as it could be a mix of scripted and conversational elements. I was happy to cheerlead for one of my best friends and suggested a limited series podcast.

"Perfect," Tara said. "I'll send over some information. Introduce you to Toshi. He can give you a tour of the statues." Now, I'd already seen the statues. They were amazing and seemed so random out there, sprinkled in between the trees. But when I opened the files that Tara sent, I realized that I hadn't really seen them at all. Just like Toshi, I understood *there was a message*.

Backstory: Chauncey Stillman was born in 1907, the middle of three children in a family that was swimming in success and wealth. His grandfather had been a railroad tycoon and president of what would become Citibank. His father was one of the largest benefactors of Harvard University. They lived in a mansion on the Upper East Side of Manhattan, and all was well. But grief spares no one, not even the wealthy. At eighteen years old, while Chauncey was away at Harvard, his mother died. His father died less than a year later. Still reeling from this loss, Chauncey would lose his baby brother, Eliot, two short years after that, in 1928. His grave would be inscribed with the Bible passage Isaiah 33:17: "His eyes shall see the King in His beauty. They shall behold a land of far distances."

Chauncey was twenty-one when he and his older sister, Elizabeth, became orphans. Chauncey would graduate and go on to receive a master's degree in architecture, travel through Europe, and fall under the spell of Greek mythology, while beginning a lifelong love affair with conservation and progressive land management. The Dust Bowl of the 1930s alarmed Stillman, and so in 1937 he launched a magazine called *Free America* that encouraged patronage and the sharing of wealth throughout agricultural communities. He started an organization that funded scientific research focusing on horticulture and biology, with the goal of improving economic and social lives in rural areas. His philosophy boiled down to "spread the wealth." Stillman was an educated lover of art, and he didn't want to hoard it for himself. Sharing land and beauty and knowledge was all a part of his homesteading dream. And so, in the same year he launched his magazine, he would purchase a few depleted dairy farms spanning four hundred acres in Dutchess County, New York. Unlike other elite New York families such as the Rockefellers and Vanderbilts, Stillman didn't buy his land on the banks of the river where all his wealth could be paraded to passing ships and trains. He tucked it away in a community that needed infrastructure and opportunity. He knew that he could put his idealism to work and create an entire economy of jobs. He continued purchasing land until the property was about twelve hundred acres.

In January 1939, he would marry Theodora and break ground on Wethersfield, finally on his way to creating a family like the one he'd loved and lost. Their daughter Emily was born in October of that same year and would only live thirteen days. I've been open about my own struggles with miscarriages, and Tara had been the friend to hold my hand and coach me through those losses. Learning that her grandfather's life was marred by such a devastating death after experiencing an avalanche of grief as a teenager, I understood his need to create something to fill the void and quiet the mind.

Years would pass before the Stillmans would have more children, two daughters in rapid succession right at the tail end of World War II. Serving in the US Navy as an air combat intelligence officer, Chauncey joined the federal government's newly formed Defense Department and would soon be transferred to the Central Intelligence Agency, where not even modern-day FOIA requests will divulge what he was up to. All the while, he was using that architecture degree to design the house and gardens and reforest the land.

But his marriage couldn't survive. Death and war and unrelenting schedules are powerful obstacles. And by 1949, Chauncey was alone again. His solace was his sister, Aunt Lizzie to his girls. Their long correspondences have been preserved and they have a Hansel and Gretel quality, reflecting the experiences of two abandoned children left to make sense of the woods. Tragedy persisted, and by 1956, Lizzie was gone too.

How does any person process the universal truth that everyone you love will die one day? For something that is a natural part of life, we are painfully ill equipped to face death. But Chauncey Stillman was dealt a particularly bad hand. And this was an era in which men weren't encouraged to share their feelings. *Therapy? What was that?*

Chauncey turned to the garden.

The following decades were spent commissioning extensive statuary to populate not just the gardens, but the fields and forest as well. I suppose I'd always just assumed that Mr. Stillman had picked up the statues here and there during his travels abroad. Learning that every one of them was a specific request changed my perception. Each Greek or Roman god reflected a chapter in Stillman's life. Armed with this new knowledge, I sat down with Toshi to interview him for the podcast.

This was a family affair. Tara's sister Miranda is a podcast producer, and she did all the recording. We'd met outside Wethersfield and bonded over haunted houses, ghost tours, and witchy stuff, and we knew that we would be friends right away.

We sat down at Wethersfield's endless dining room table with floor-to-ceiling oil portraits of Chauncey and his sister watching over us, and I confessed to Toshi that I knew nothing of Italian Renaissance gardens. He explained the notion that the garden actually began in the depths of the woods, in "darker, more mystical spaces that they called Bosci." These wooded parts of the garden were thought of as pagan spaces, and the statues there were pre-Christian, Greek mythological figures. The statuary was arranged along a path in order to tell a story. Sometimes that was a universal story of civilization, and sometimes it was a deeply personal narrative about the owner of the estate. You would wind your way through the Bosci and emerge in the formal garden. Toshi explained, "It would show what humanity could accomplish when working with God to overcome this sort of darker mystical woodland garden."

Toshi had spent his first winter at Wethersfield trying to decode the story of the statues.

"Mr. Stillman was a classicist; he was well-traveled, well-read; he knew the Italian gardens and what they meant. I knew that these weren't just random statues dotted around the woods and I thought it must be some kind of journey. But I didn't have the classical education. So I would Google things: *Who were these statues? How are they related?*"

The first key Toshi had was a blueprint for a set of steps that descended into the woods designed by Stillman's landscape architect, Evelyn Poehler. She called them "The Steps to Dorcas." In the Bible, Dorcas was a widow who was brought back from the dead by St. Peter. Toshi saw the connection between the plans and the personal history of the family. "Now, the blueprints were made in 1971. And Mr. Stillman, he was divorced. But his ex-wife had died in 1968. So, he was a widower too. And so I wondered, *Is he Dorcas? Is he the figure who's somehow died and been reborn? Is the wilderness his story?* There's this notion that the garden was maybe his personal journey, some kind of spiritual journey."

The second key was a scavenger hunt that Mr. Stillman had created for the property, on which he sent people to find the "Entrance to Orcas." At first Toshi thought it was an alternate spelling for Dorcas, or just a good old-fashioned typo, but it turns out Orcas is a Roman deity of the Underworld. The themes of death and rebirth kept surfacing. Toshi came across a famous passage in Virgil's *Aeneid*, where Aeneas is searching for his dead father and enters the Underworld through, you guessed it, the Jaws of Orcas! Virgil describes another creature that lurks in the Underworld, the centaur. Toshi continued, "Sure enough, one of the first statues you see after you enter the gates, the Entrance to Orcas, is a centaur, and it's *massive*. Apparently, it was carved from a two-ton piece of stone."

I remembered my first time walking the woods with Tara and seeing the centaur rising out of the brush. I was drawn to the creature, its intimidating stature juxtaposed with the tiny details of frogs and turtles delicately carved at the statue's base. The statue gives off a dull sense of alarm. Its intention was to subconsciously disorient you. If something like that can exist in these woods, anything goes.

At our next meeting, Toshi took me on a private tour of the three separate gardens, Inferno, Purgatory, and Paradise. The first thing we encountered was a shady glade of nymphs called the Nemara. They peeked out from the trees, staring back at the house. Hidden just beyond their depths was a thick tangle of ferns. Smack dab in the middle of their feathery leaves was a life-size statue of a leopard. Random? Perhaps. Unless you know a little about Dante's *Divine Comedy*, where Dante and Virgil make their way through the circles of Hell, the hard work of Purgatory, and the reward of Paradise. At the very beginning of the journey,

Dante heads straight for Heaven, but is confronted by three beasts: a lion that represents pride, a she-wolf that represents greed, and a leopard that represents lust. These beasts block Dante's path and send him on his way to Hell in the very same way this predatory cat positions herself to send you down a descending garden path in the woods.

The next statue is Atalanta, coupled with her partner, Melanion. Atalanta was a legendary huntress and the only female Argonaut, modeling herself after the goddess Artemis. She loved her work and intended to stay a virgin like the goddess, but Melanion fell in love with her and asked the love goddess Aphrodite to help him win the hand of his crush. To this purpose, Aphrodite gave him golden apples. Atalanta said she would only marry a man who could beat her in a race, and she was confident in her ability to win when Melanion challenged her. But during the race, he threw the golden apples in her direction, distracting her, and he was able to finish the victor. Theirs was a happy marriage. That is, until Aphrodite got annoyed that he never thanked her for the apples and cursed them with eternal separation.

It's a story not too dissimilar to that of Chauncey Stillman's parents. His mother had been a career girl working as a nurse when his father was injured and fell in love with her while under her care. Like Melanion and Atalanta, they had a happy marriage, and their early deaths felt very much like a curse.

This is where the garden path diverges. To the left is a massive Palladian arch, and beyond it a stretch of land dubbed the Elysian Fields. In mythology, the Greeks regarded the Elysian Fields as the final resting place for their heroes. Toshi explained the structure to me.

"There's an inscription in the arch from Isaiah, which says,

'Thine eyes shall see the glory of the King. And you shall see great distances.' And you think when you first see it, *Oh, that's a perfect description for Wethersfield.* You're at the top of this hill and you're in this glorious space. But, I was doing some research again into Mr. Stillman's life, and I came across this image of his little brother's grave. And on the grave was that same inscription, '*His eyes shall see the King in His beauty . . .*' And so, you get this sense that this field is like a memorial field. And then the statues along the side of it sort of fell into place as well. They represent his parents and represent himself. Between Virgil and Dante, I think you have the story of the garden."

Again and again as I walked those paths, I thought of Mr. Johnson and the kick he would have gotten as we decoded the significance of the statuary and uncovered these testaments to Mr. Stillman's life.

Toshi led me farther down the path, heading toward the Gates of Orcus. I noticed a consistent hedge, massive in height, planted along the entire wood line. "What is that?" I asked him.

"Oh, that? It's burning bush. Later in the season that will become bright red and orange." Inferno, indeed.

As you approach the gates, they are jarring. They're an unnatural thing to stumble upon in the woods, and your brain knows intuitively to be on high alert. They soar up, stone pillars with large carved hawks perched on them. In Greek mythology, hawks were the messengers of Apollo. One of the pillars bears the Latin inscription found in Dante's *Inferno*: *Lasciate ogne Speranza, voi ch'intrante.* "Abandon all hope, ye who enter here."

Beyond the ominous gates, there is a fountain, with a reflecting pool I thought nothing of letting our kids wade in during the oppressive summer months. Turns out it is a symbol for the nine circles of Hell, with more cyclical paths building off of it. *Cool, cool.*

Continuing on, one finds the bittersweet embrace of Orpheus and Eurydice. Orpheus had been a poet and musician and was set to be married to the wood nymph Eurydice. A tragedy sent her to the Underworld, but Orpheus followed her down and talked Hades and Persephone into letting his beloved go. However, there was one condition: Orpheus had to walk straight out of Hell and never look back to see if Eurydice was following him. Poor guy; he couldn't do it. Right as they were about to emerge from Hell, he glanced back, and his beloved was sent back to the Underworld forever. Orpheus never recovered from the loss. It's a parable that doesn't sound terribly different from a marriage racked by grief. Had Chauncey gone down into the depths of despair with his wife and tried to emerge with her as a unit, only to fall apart?

The path continues to circle in the woods, and the next thing on the journey is the aforementioned centaur. Legends say that centaurs guarded the circles of Hell, specifically the seventh circle, said to house murderers and those prone to violence on earth. I asked Tara if her grandfather had experienced violence in his lifetime.

"Oh, in the war? Sure. He was horrified by that experience." He had in fact written a letter to his sister on the subject, on May 21, 1941:

As we have shared in the making of an unjust and violent world, we are committed to the means, the methods of that world . . . It is important, especially in these times, to pin our hope for the ultimate leadership of humanity in the spiritual, not the military.

This is the point in the journey where the path begins to ascend, and we enter Purgatory. The deeper our little gang got into the world of mythology, the clearer it became that we needed an expert, our own guide through the Underworld. Tara reached out to the head of Italian Studies at nearby Bard College, Professor Joe Luzzi. As a leading authority on Dante's works, Joe provided context for the different parts of the garden. While Hell was despair, Purgatory actually represented hope. There was work to do in Purgatory. You could improve yourself through introspection and spiritual devotion in hopes that you would eventually ascend to Heaven. The path into Mr. Stillman's personal Purgatory was steep, and lined on either side by laurel bushes. These are the leaves that young athletes would be crowned with in antiquity. Waiting for us at the crest of that hill was, in fact, a teen boy: a commissioned replica of the Hiram Powers statue *Fisher Boy*, found in the Metropolitan Museum of Art. It is clearly a very young man, with a net in his hand. But on all maps of Wethersfield, this stop was labeled "Poseidon." And who was Poseidon? God of the Seas, cohort of Apollo and protector of seafarers. As Mr. Stillman had been in the navy during the war, did he feel looked after by this deity? We know that he paid tribute to his brother's memory in the Elysian Fields, but was this statue a tribute to the physical boy? Curiously, when one looks up *Fisher Boy*, the artist cites Apollo as the inspiration for the sculpture. So, what was Mr. Stillman up to? Much the same way world mythology and modern religions absorb and overlap similar characters, could he have been merging multiple gods to create a sense of who his little brother was? What was the overlap between Poseidon and Apollo?

As you continue along, Diana and Hippolytus flank either side of the path. Also known as Artemis by the Greeks (remember her from the Atalanta story?), the Romans worshipped Diana as the goddess of the hunt, a virtuous heroine often surrounded by wood nymphs. Her first head priest, Hippolytus, was a hunter and sportsman who rejected sex. This pissed Aphrodite off and she cursed him, eventually bringing about his death. He was resurrected from the dead, and spent the rest of his time leading the cult of Artemis.

"Who are these people supposed to be?" I'd asked Toshi and Tara.

"We're not totally sure yet," Tara replied.

"I mean, Chauncey's sister was his most trusted confidante. He worshipped her. And Diana is such a powerful entity. Is this them?" It felt like unsealing a long forgotten letter, a message from beyond. There was a lesson here in the work of Purgatory, about overcoming the lust of earthly desires and material goals. Diana and Hippolytus had cast those things off. They valued nature and little else.

The next stop, and final statue of Purgatory, was Hercules. Son of Zeus and a mortal, and all-around golden boy, Hercules is basically the Jesus of Greek mythology. When he died, his father made him a god and had him ascend to Mount Olympus. He is representative of doing the hard work of living in order to assume one's place in Heaven in the afterlife. As the final statue of the wilderness garden, he is large and gorgeous, and a reward to see after the taxing hike.

"Where do we go now?" I asked Toshi. The trail ended. This is where Mr. Stillman's guests would climb down from his impressive carriage and enter the garden of Paradise on foot. There are no Greek gods in the formal garden. It is a heaven made of flowers and the artistry of nature, with vistas that seem like oil paintings from the Old Masters. It all is lit up by the breathtaking sky vault described in Dante's Paradiso. It is light. Dawns and dusks, starshine and moonshine and fireflies across the fields. There is magic here. There is pain turned to beauty.

Chauncey Stillman, a man capable of passing down a sizeable inheritance to his ancestors, went a step further and created a personal mythology that he married to the universal mythology of antiquity. Our truths will be eternal. It was, I realized, his grimoire. Only no one had known this until now.

"Did your grandfather ever talk in code?" I'd asked Tara on the hike.

"Of course! For Valentine's Day, he would give us calligraphy valentines in mirror writing. You could only read them reflected in a mirror. I think it was a deeply engrained love of puzzles and mystery from his days in the CIA."

It would seem that Mr. Stillman left one last love letter, not just to his family, but to the greater Hudson Valley. On his deathbed, he entrusted the estate to the public, so that everything he built could be enjoyed by others.

Tara waxed on this idea. "There's really something extraordinarily important about beauty in dark times. Because as we go through dark times, sometimes you're by yourself. It's more personal. But if there's a large-scale crisis or some kind of international crisis or a war or a *pandemic*, you start looking for beautiful things because they're like oxygen, right? If every day, everything is just full-on dark, it's just too much. You have to find these things that just get you through. And so, Wethersfield, to me, is that invitation to come and find what's beautiful."

THAT NIGHT, I STOOD MAKING DINNER FOR MY KIDS IN THE kitchen, head swimming with myths and gods and the very real history of my best friend's family. How did it all connect? Apollo's name had come up time and time again. Gus was in the thick of his sixth-grade Greek god studies—fortuitous timing! "Kid," I said as he breezed past me on the way to the fridge. "What do you know about Apollo?"

He paused. "Apollo? That's the guy who rides around in the chariot. Twin brother of Diana."

That's it! I thought. Chauncey, the carriage aficionado, had cast himself as Apollo. He'd built monuments to his brother and parents as Atalanta and Melonian in the Elysian Fields. He'd placed a centaur—most likely Chiron, Apollo's wise tutor—in the middle of Inferno, along with the heartbreaking story of Apollo's son Orpheus's marriage gone wrong. Adolescent-looking *Fisher Boy* was little brother Eliot. Diana, twin to Apollo, *was* a representation of his sister Lizzie. The same way I had seen myself in Medusa, Mr. Stillman made sense of the tragic stories in his life by looking toward antiquity. It's a soothing practice. We cry out in pain and the echoes bounce back to us through thousands of years: "You are not alone. Many have stood here. Even the gods."

Goddesses, Gods, Saints, and Such

It is the loss of the feminine counterpart of God that causes the wound that never heals.

—Margaret Starbird

*T*he gods and goddesses are all around us; all you have to do is pick one, or two, or a pantheon to worship and draw strength from when the spirit moves you. I thought about the multitude of ways we keep the deities close when I took Gus and George to a Renaissance Faire, where Gus's friend J. J.'s family had a patch of land devoted to the Vikings. J. J.'s mom, Rebecca, who is an ex-military, marathon-running goddess herself, showed us the Viking tents, the traditional kitchen, the forge, and functional gardens they used throughout faire season. Her pride and joy was a space dedicated to the Norse gods she had created, with logs carved to look like totem poles, displaying the likenesses of Loki, Freya, and Baldur and their cohorts. There, amid the horses and armor and leather goods, you could pause in front of the divine.

When I was trying to get pregnant with George, I lit a candle in front of a statue of the Black Madonna in Barcelona. For a decade, I wore a necklace with a Saint Brigid medal before learning that she is the Celtic and Christian version of Persephone. And some nights I just howl at my girlfriend, the moon. Inviting the sacred in has given me solace and strength and peace. For too long, witchcraft had been defined as the *division* of women and faith, suggesting that witches are heathens. In reality witchcraft is about profound faith and deep inspiration from the lessons of God, goddesses, gods, and nature. No matter your preference of faith, there is a supreme being for you. Whether you find grace in churches, temples, or the vast wildness of creation, if you haven't already discovered your special someone, here are a few candidates for your altar.

KALI is the Hindu goddess of ultimate power, time, destruction, death, and change. She is regarded as the ultimate manifestation of Shakti, the primordial cosmic energy, and the mother of all living beings. She vanquishes evil to safeguard the innocent, bestows liberation, and brings balance to the divine feminine and masculine forces. She is also linked with sexuality, violence, and even, sometimes, with motherly love. She is usually depicted in black or blue, mostly naked, with a long tongue, a multitude of arms, and a necklace of decapitated heads while gripping another decapitated head in her hand as she dances or stands atop her husband, the god Shiva.

BRIGID was a Celtic goddess in Ireland before Christianity was a flicker in its green eye. Her cult was powerful, and her devotees were too faithful to forsake her, so the Celtic Christian Church and then the Roman Catholic Church were forced to adopt her and make her a saint. She is a guardian of livestock and the young, a patroness of poetry, metalwork, healing, and spring, and, alongside St. Patrick, is the patron saint of Ireland.

DIONYSUS is my son Gus's favorite Greek god. Seriously. I asked him while I was making notes for this book and his exact quote was, "Dionysus! That's my guy!" I hope it is not because he is the deity of wine and ecstasy, but rather because he is young, gorgeous, and boisterous. Dionysus, known as Bacchus in the Roman pantheon, is the god of fruitfulness and vegetation, which includes the grape vine. As the god of good times, sumptuous feasts are one of the best ways to honor him.

KUAN YIN is a Buddhist goddess of compassion and mercy. Her name translates to "perceiving the sounds (or cries) of the world." Her calling to alleviate suffering has made her a symbol of vegetarianism. Her followers bring her offerings like sweet cakes, lotus incense, and fresh fruit or flowers, especially when they hope to conceive.

ISIS is the most powerful deity in the Egyptian pantheon, believed to heal the sick and bring back the dead. Her name means "seat," as in throne, because she was the ultimate mom—a giving mother and protectress, who is thought of as the mother of all the pharaohs. She was also known as "the Great Magic" and "Mother of the Gods" and became so beloved that she was the only god worshipped by the entire country; the other gods were demoted to mere aspects of her. Her clergy was peopled with both men and women, and the Cult of Isis was rumored to hold the secrets of life and death, but its followers were sworn to secrecy.

COYOTE is a divine being for many Native American tribes. He is the chief animal of the age before humans and the one who gave humans the gift of fire, daylight, and the arts. Coyote, like all of us, embodies his duality—he is known as both a cultural hero of wisdom and light and a classic bad boy who exemplifies the perils of avarice, recklessness, and arrogance. He is crafty and intelligent, a magician, a glutton, a creator, a lover, and a transgressive force that instigates social and physical chaos.

FREYA is the Norse goddess of love and fertility, with a reputation for being a bit of a party girl. She is also the pre-eminent practitioner of the Norse magic called *seidr*, delivering the practice to both the gods and humans. Her ability to control and manipulate desires, health, and the riches of others leaves her with unrivaled power. She is also associated with the dead, as she presides over Folkvang, a meadow in the afterlife where fallen warriors were brought. She is believed to help guide the dead into the afterlife. If you leave her offerings of mead, honey, and meat, she may just help you attract love or practice magic.

PACHAMAMA is the Earth Mother of Inca mythology, and the Mother Earth goddess worshipped by the Andean people. Her shrines are in hollowed-out rocks or carved-out tree trunks. After the Spanish imposed Catholicism on the indigenous people, they fused Pachamama with Mary, Mother of God. Pachamama is the goddess of nourishment and abundance and the embodiment of all of creation. She reminds me a lot of the Greek goddess Gaia, another one of my favorites. She is associated with rituals for fertility, protection, and healthy crops. She appreciates offerings from the land—food, tobacco, coca leaves, and a little libation now and then.

ST. FRANCIS OF ASSISI is the patron saint of animals, merchants, and ecology, but he was not always a modest man. He was a handsome and highfalutin young fella, born into the lap of luxury until he heard the voice of God, who commanded him to rebuild the Christian church and to live in poverty. St. Francis is known for his compassion for the vulnerable, especially the poor, the infirm, and animals.

OYA is one of the great feminine spirits called the Orisha in the Yoruba religion of West Africa. The goddess of storms, winds, rainbows, and thunder, and a water goddess of the Niger River, she is a fierce warrior, known for protecting women and her use of charms and magic. She also goes by the epic title "Great Mother of the Elders of the Night," or, in Haitian Voodoo circles, Yansa.

TARA is the Buddhist goddess who appears in Nepal, Tibet, and Mongolia. In Sanskrit, her name means "the one who takes you across." She is the protectress of navigation and earthly travel, as well as of spiritual travel along the path to enlightenment, and is the feminine counterpart of the bodhisattva. There are many incarnations of Tara. In her fierce, blue form she is called upon to destroy enemies; in red, she is a goddess of love. She can also be Janguli, protectress against snake bites, or the yellow Tara with the furious brows. White Tara symbolizes the day, and is associated with grace, serenity, and motherly love. Tibetan Buddhists pray to her for healing and longevity. Green Tara symbolizes the night, and is associated with activity and abundance; people petition her for wealth and protection on journeys, as well as freedom from delusions or negative emotions.

FLOWER POWER

y the time March is through, my patience for slush and snow and ice and gray skies has worn thin. And so, when I spy the first little crocuses that peek out of the snow, I know they are sentinels come to save my sanity.

Then come those little grape-looking plants, mini hyacinths. Daffodils brighten things up right after that. Then the tulips emerge, followed quickly by the lilac here. There's an enormous lilac bush at the corner of my house that reminds me of the lilac fort I had as a child back on Ithaca. I throw the windows wide open during their bloom so that the house is filled with my comfort scent from childhood. Lilacs on Ithaca are a sense memory that never fades.

Behind the lilac parade is the azaleas. I have one hot-pink one here at the farm as a reminder of my years in Wilmington. Anyone who has been through there knows that the Azalea Festival is a sight to behold—literally an entire holiday weekend dedicated to the electric-pink and purple blossoms that coat the coastal city. If you've always wanted to visit Wilmington, make it your bucket-list goal to go to Airlie Gardens during Azalea Festival. It's a fairy kingdom every dreamer should walk through.

After the azaleas come the peonies, and these are my favorite. I'd never been able to grow peonies before moving to the Hudson Valley, and I was kind of intimidated by the process. But when we bought the farm in October 2013, the previous owner, Sunny, gave me a heads-up that the month of May would be pretty glorious here at the farm. She had planted peony roots all along the back of the house. What a gorgeous thing to inherit! Those lush velvet petals and their deep feminine fragrance make me feel a certain way.

And I think that's what the best flowers do. They make us feel a certain way.

It is pleasure just to witness them. It is pleasure to be around them. It is pleasure to leave them exactly where they are. That's not to say I won't cut a few, bring them into the house, and put them in a mason jar next to my bed. But the beauty of the flower orchestra is that as one beautiful thing dies out, another is quickly taking its place. And this repeats week by week.

After the peonies, there are lilies, a riot of orange and burgundy and yellow. Then the zinnias start popping like fireworks in their variety of vibrant shades.

The black-eyed Susans show up around the same time and soon after that, my marigolds. I don't wanna brag, but my Mischief marigolds take over and can carry us all the way through Halloween. We make our Day of the Dead crowns and decorate altars to lost loved ones. One of my dearest friends, film director James Ponsoldt, hosts the most wonderful annual gathering in LA with a group of his friends. They invite everyone in their circle to a Día de los Muertos party, where a shrine is set up and anyone can add photos, treasures, and mementos for the people that they have loved and lost. That's such an essential gathering for humans to be able to have, where we can collectively share in our grief and our love, even if it's not for the same people. It's important to know that those emotions are universal and perfectly okay to express. At our wedding in October 2019, we gave away marigold seeds to everyone who came, so that they could take a piece of our farm home with them.

The hydrangeas are obscene here at the farm. They show up midsummer and go from vibrant blue to lavender to pink to white, and then their petals slowly thin until they are ghostly wisps of their former selves. Those dried-out flowers last all winter long. And I don't cut them until late spring, when new buds finally appear.

Last year we added bee balm around our garden, and my husband was smitten. He loved it for its firework-red blooms. But it's also ancient medicine that fixes everything from nausea and sore throats to bee stings and rashes.

Magic, real honest-to-goodness magic, is about acknowledging the power of the natural world. It is about respecting not just the divinity in humans, but in every living thing.

ON AUGUST 7, 2021, I'D WOKEN UP EARLY ON CAPE COD AND MOVED about in the silence of my family sleeping, marveling at what a perfectly gorgeous day it was. The night before, I'd seen shooting stars for the first time in my life. The trip had been a dreamy experience. A breeze toyed with the old roller shade at the window, bringing coolness and salt air. We packed our cars to check out by 10 a.m.

after spending a blissful family week in a new place, Sagamore Beach. And as I loaded suitcases and clothes hampers, I walked back and forth along a row of rosebushes. Most blossoms had turned to hips, but the remaining flowers were velvety scented, and I can recall saying out loud, "I love it here." That rose scent remained with me a few hours into my drive home.

My phone buzzed. Megan Park, one of my dearest friends, texted: *Can you talk? It's important.*

I told her I was on the road and to call anytime.

Are the kids with you?

No, I answered. *They drove in dad's fun car.*

"Are you okay?" I asked when she finally called.

"Yes, I'm good. We're all good." But then she told me. *Markie.* I'd known she'd been sick. But as uncomplaining and bright and involved as she was, I thought she'd gotten better. I messed up.

I didn't want to linger on the phone, and Megan is a good enough friend that we can be ourselves in those kinds of moments. The flood of tears hit after we hung up.

Markie had played my mother in a Christmas movie when Gus was three. We'd fallen madly in love, and had a blissful summer being a pretend family. Tyler Hilton, Megan, Markie, and I were joined at the hip. We collected inside jokes, wore harmonicas in town, drank Skinnygirl margaritas from Walmart, and smoked secret cigarettes like bad kids. Markie was so easy to be with. It is hard to elaborate here, because writing about her in the past tense feels sad.

The week Jeffrey and I finally packed up the house in LA and sold it, Markie invited Megan, Tyler, and me to her house in Toluca Lake for dinner with her and her husband, Michael. The edge of her property was lined with a stately brick wall absolutely swimming in roses. Enviable, perfect blooms. I'd never been able to grow roses before. They're a bit picky. They need attention and love to be coaxed out. But Markie was good at that stuff. She brushed off the compliments on her garden and ushered us into her home, where feminine florals continued throughout the décor. It was like moving through an impeccable dollhouse. She quickly brought us back to her pride and joy: her craft room. Costumes, curtains, pillows, gifts—Markie was a maker, a creator.

I HAD THIS PHRASE I ALWAYS USED TO UNDERCUT MYSELF: *I make poor choices*. The first time I'd said it in front of Markie, she burst out laughing and said, "I love poor choices!" So, from this craft room, Markie produced a pillow she had made just for me. Pale cream, with girly floral and diamond accents. It said "What fun is life without a few poor choices?" My god, she got it!

I knew Markie's daughters, Kate and Daisy, understood how beloved their mom was. They told stories about the fairy gardens Markie would build them, and the years of notes those fairies would leave them under pillows and for birthdays and any other occasion that needed some extra bolstering. I was devastated by her loss. I was more than that. I was angry. So many assholes in the world, and this beautiful, generous, magical human was gone?

I went out to my garden as soon as I got home. Only one week away, and it was alive with weeds and food ready to be picked. I worked until it was set right again, hands and nails caked with dirt. Putting pain to work has always been my best medicine. But then, I wanted a memory of the day.

A tangible memory of Markie that I could keep along with my "Poor Choices" pillow.

The previous fall, I had planted rosebushes along the perimeter of my garden. They sat dormant all winter, all spring, and most of the summer. But I'd been babying them, learning what made them happy. And upon returning home, there were a dozen fully open roses with a significant number of buds on deck. After all this time, I was a step closer to being like this woman I so admired. So, I cut the two most beautiful flowers there: a yellow rose and a powder-pink cabbage rose. I brought them inside and prepared to press them between the pages of a book back in my office, when a dark something caught my eye in the heart of the dense pink petals. Pulling them apart, I saw a lone bee, skinny with faded coloring and moving solemnly slow. Jeff looked on. He knew I was heartbroken and kept checking in on me. "Poor guy doesn't have long," he said.

I did not press the rose that night. Instead, I sat with that flower—like the main character in *The Little Prince*—and let the bee slowly poke its head out and brush its antenna up against my finger.

My bee fell asleep in time, in the gorgeous scented bed of rose petals.

What did this sign mean? It was comfort. The news of my friend's passing had been abrupt. I felt like I was choking.

But, Markie was a rose. A total showstopper. Soft and stunning. A flower we've all grown up with and one that feels familiar. Watching this rose give comfort to this fading honeybee . . . it forced me to stop and bear witness and acknowledge the universal fact that loving means losing eventually, and that being your softest self is sometimes all you can do.

I want to be a rose woman like Markie.

And each year, as I witness the symphony of my flowers, I am continually moved by the idea that as one beloved thing enters its season of loss, another is blooming.

Secret Language of Flowers

Women have always been healers. They were the unlicensed doctors and anatomists. They were abortionists, nurses and counselors. They were the pharmacists, cultivating healing herbs, and exchanging the secrets of their uses. They were midwives, traveling from home to home and village to village. For centuries women were doctors without degrees, barred from books and lectures, learning from each other, and passing on experience from neighbor to neighbor and mother to daughter. They were called "wise women" by the people, witches or charlatans by the authorities. Medicine is part of our heritage as women, our history, our birthright.

—Barbara Ehrenreich and Deirdre English, *Witches, Midwives and Nurses: A History of Women Healers*

*D*arlin', did you know that flowers have a language? Did you know that you could use them like a decoder ring to send secret messages to your friends and loved ones? It's an age-old practice and one that we probably take for granted. I feel like I've always known that yellow roses were for friendship or that red flowers were lusty. We're fairly particular about what flowers we send to funerals, and those end up being very different from the flowers that we send to our valentines or for birthdays or the blossoms we use at weddings.

Are you a fan of monochromatic arrangements, or are you sending deeply layered meanings with mixed bouquets? The Victorians were particularly good at this. They could wear a flower on the lapel of a jacket or the brim of a hat that projected their mood or intentions to the greater community. I wish we still wore flowers. How cool would that be? To be able to see the mindset of all the other mothers in the school pickup line projected like an aura through the flowers they wore on their Lululemon and parkas.

Uh-oh! Kimberly is wearing alyssum to ward off anger! Watch out!

Do I start this trend? I feel like it's a modest luxury that we should absolutely bring back.

We all know plants are magic. Flowers in food not only add to the aesthetics of the creation, but they impart medicinal properties as well. The idea that a flower can heal me is exactly what I wanted to believe in as a little girl. And so, finding out in adulthood that it is a *reality*? How thrilling!

It's no secret I am partial to dandelions. Their detoxifying capabilities are legendary. And as I look out my window right now there is a sea of them in the yard. Sunshine on a stem.

What other plants in your yard are full of potential?

Mint, with its tiny purple flowers, means virtue and brings a brightness to everything from mixed drinks to curry. And peppermint is known to conjure prophetic dreams and bring change. Spearmint is known for spiritual cleansing and to dispel that pesky evil eye.

Rose hips' sour tang can be used in healing spells and for good luck.

Echinacea's blooms help with pain and inflammation, and its witchy properties include adding power and drawing money.

Calendula flower is an antioxidant and anti-inflammatory. It can be used for protection, to address legal matters, and to strengthen justice.

Nasturtiums, with their peppery taste, are the perfect flowers to add to salads, while they also stand for victory in battle.

And if you have a raspberry bush, harvest the leaves and blend them with hyssop and mint to make a tonic for women. Its witchy uses include healing and love.

Squash flowers are a delicacy introduced to me by my dearest manager and chosen family, Meg Mortimer. Her husband, David, is a foodie who has introduced me to all sorts of fine things in life like turducken, goat cheese, and the aforementioned squash blossoms. The symbol of squash blossoms has been used to ward off the evil eye or indicate prosperity.

Joy Lenz puts pink rose petals—a symbol of happiness—in her cocktails, causing Sophia Bush and I to immediately fall under her spell. Have you ever put rose water in your baking? It's a must. Sharagim also knows I'm a sucker for roses. She spoils me with Iranian *noghl*, which is almonds coated in sugar and rose water. It is pure love, in candied form.

You can eat lilies right off the stem, and those have as many different meanings as they do colors!

Tea is a surefire way to incorporate your garden into your diet. Every Christmas, Gus makes specially curated blends of tea for members of the family, dear friends, and beloved teachers. We get create-your-own tea bags, and he fills them from the botanical-filled mason jars that line our kitchen island. There is jasmine, pink rose petals, lavender, dandelion root (which is less bitter than the greens), vanilla bean snipped into tiny pieces, and hibiscus, which is his very favorite. From our garden (Gus has always been my garden helper, while George gravitates toward the animals) we have calming chamomile and soothing mint, harvested and dried. Gus and I talk about the colors and healing properties and he sets about filling the bags with blends that soothe, detoxify, and heal. Watching him fill old tin canisters and ceramic vessels with these little packages of care, I'm struck with pride to see my witchy kid brewing up potions for the people he loves.

Whether you eat them, drink them, or arrange them, flowers speak. I'm a flower talker, and I love poring through books that explain what each flower means.

Here are some highlights to get you started:

+ Send aloe to soothe grief.
+ Begonia says beware! (I love having this planted by the front door to give unwanted guests a heads-up!)
+ Black-eyed Susans mean justice.
+ Carnations are symbolic of female love, between mothers and daughters, sisters, and dear friends.

+ Daffodils embody respect and high regard.
+ Ferns hint at the secret bonds of love and magical thinking.
+ Gardenias say you're beautiful!
+ Hydrangeas express gratitude for being understood. (Mischief Farm is swimming in these!)
+ Lavender means distrust.
+ Peonies are bashful.
+ "Rosemary for remembrance" is a classic quote from Alice Hoffman's *Magic Lessons*.
+ Tall sunflowers indicate haughtiness.
+ Red tulips are a passionate declaration of love.
+ And perhaps I care so much for zinnias because they represent lasting affection and thoughts of absent friends.

Use your flower fluency to encode a message in a bouquet for a lover, a friend, or maybe even a long-buried loved one. Or place one in your grimoire to record a feeling that can best be expressed through flowers. For more information on flower power, check out Farmer's Almanacs. They are among my favorite witchy resources! Or brew up a batch of tea. Here's one of my special blends:

Mary Magdalene Tea

¼ teaspoon mugwort also known as St. John's plant
(Artemisia vulgaris)
¼ teaspoon hibiscus
1 cardamom seed
1 teaspoon dandelion leaves
¼ teaspoon dandelion root

FIND YOUR MUSE

I became a bit fixated on muses in my early twenties, because to be perfectly frank, I wanted one.

Whom was I making art for? What did I want to capture? I lived in a sleepy little town. And so, I pored over books trying to find the answer. Since then, I've had a number of muses, other women who I think are just so fucking electric that I want to create something that lives up to the energy they put out into the world.

I don't believe you need to be an artist to have a muse. I know lawyers who have deep appreciation for other members of the legal community like Ruth Bader Ginsburg. My bestie, Sharagim, is a doctor who is deeply inspired by other doctors she sees out there. Chefs obviously have muses. Look at *Ratatouille*! And how many of us have looked at Martha Stewart and thought, "Daaaaamn!"

The definition of *muse* deserves an overhaul. Typically, there's a

kind of misogynistic conception that a muse is a woman who exists
solely to inspire a male artist, and we have a lot of examples of that.
There's Emilie Louise Flöge, depicted in so many of Gustav Klimt's
paintings. Zelda Fitzgerald. One of my favorites, Lou Andreas-
Salomé, was a muse for Nietzsche, Freud, *and* Rainer Maria Rilke.
(I'll have what she's having!) These women were mysterious and
dynamic. And if you want to learn about some of them, you should
read the book *The Lives of the Muses* by Francine Prose.

But my understanding of what a muse could be was totally
upended in the early 2000s, when two biographies hit bookstores
at the same time, both about Edna St. Vincent Millay.

Who was this woman? I was always a dork for poetry, but
somehow Edna had escaped my awareness. As I read about her, I
found a voice and style that was classical in form, yet scandalous—
and at times downright erotic—in subject matter. We all know I'm
partial to bawdy women. Her life seemed pulled from a storybook.
Here was this young woman, a total witch, living a fairy tale. Hers
was a feral childhood in New England. Edna's mother divorced
her useless husband and was a hardworking breadwinner, raising
her three daughters in a home that was deeply bohemian. Young
Edna—this teenager with the extravagant name—is the real-life Jo
March from *Little Women*. She decided to start writing poetry and
entering contests. But did she start writing about some boy she had
a crush on or some future full of white picket fences and chubby
children bouncing on her knee?

No!

Edna St. Vincent Millay decided to start writing love poetry to
her muse. *Herself.*

I sat there and pored over verses that sang the virtues of a
beloved woman. And while it was true that Millay was decidedly

bisexual, it's clear she was writing about her own assets in poems like my personal favorite, "Witch-Wife."

Witch-Wife

She is neither pink nor pale,
And she never will be all mine;
She learned her hands in a fairy-tale,
And her mouth on a valentine.

She has more hair than she needs;
In the sun 'tis a woe to me!
And her voice is a string of colored beads,
Or steps leading into the sea.

She loves me all that she can,
And her ways to my ways resign;
But she was not made for any man,
And she never will be all mine.

It's a flirty poem, and it's self-empowering knowing that she wrote it about herself. The bold fact that she would create a narrator with a male voice to describe her own attractive qualities is just fabulous.

To the baby version of myself that existed in the early aughts, it was such an outlandish idea that you could be your own muse. Is it arrogant? I mean, girls like Millay often get labeled with that word. But if you have the ability to see the parts of yourself that you like and they inspire your creativity or your profession? Kick ass!

Here's what I want you to do. Go into your grimoire and write about yourself the way you would write about someone you're in love with. Talk about the physical qualities that are intoxicating. Talk about the behavioral aspects that you like. Do you have a loud, inviting laugh? Or are you gentle and deliberate? Are you a deeply kind person? Or do you have one of those personalities that speak truth to power even when it is difficult? There are no rules! You can be all of the above. Lord knows I love the Walt Whitman quote:

"Do I contradict myself? Very well, then I contradict myself. I am large. I contain multitudes."

Be *all* the things, my friends, and make a record of it to remind yourself in darker times how truly inspiring you are. Acknowledge your *me-gic*!

What's your "me-gic"? What is it about you that feels magical? Are you an animal-whisperer? Are you gifted at putting puzzle pieces together and helping people figure things out?

Are you a witch with a green thumb? Or a food wizard?

I did not know what my "me-gic" was until a *One Tree Hill* convention in Paris. We had a couple of meet-and-greets where a small gathering of fans got to hang out with the group. This allowed for intimate conversations, and even though there were language barriers, it was such a fun, effortless event. One fan in particular said something I will never forget. She came up to me and through broken English announced that my gift was not acting.

I must have looked very confused.

Then she said to me, "No, no. That doesn't mean you're not good at acting. But that's not your gift. Your gift is seeing people."

How curious for a stranger to say that! She told me that she'd watched me interact with people all day long. And that she had seen me in interviews with other castmates, had seen me in various projects, and she recognized that I had a steady focus on trying to make the people around me feel valued. Later, I went to my hotel room and cried because it just meant so damn much to me. So much of my value as a person had been based on acting. But in my heart of hearts, I knew it wasn't my calling. This woman saw me. She saw what I wanted to be. She acknowledged my gift, my unique magic. What an angel!

We all have something special about us, a thing deep down inside of us that is specifically ours. Our magic. Our me-gic.

I prefer to say this word with a funny accent. 'Cause, why not? I encourage you to do the same. Look at yourself in the mirror, put your hands on your hips, and announce to yourself:

"There is great magic in me.

I am creative.

I am curious.

And I am magnetic as all hell!"

It's *really* hard to pay ourselves compliments. I think we all agree on that. It feels weird to say, "Yes, that is my gift." But I credit that fan in Paris for helping me see myself differently, and for thinking that my me-gic was something worth mentioning. Of all the things she could have said to me in that short amount of time, she chose to point out my gift, one I couldn't really see yet. I'm not a strong swimmer. I'm not very good with languages. I can't ride a bicycle. I am severely lacking in a multitude of departments. But my me-gic is the thing that sees me through all those other obstacles. I may have the coordination of a newborn calf and a limited education and a hot temper, but I can see the goddamn good in everyone and everything.

If you don't know what the me-gic is in you, the easiest way to find it out is to compliment other people by telling them what their own me-gic is. Your friends need to hear it. Your loved ones need to hear it. Tell them what quality of theirs stands out as being special. And chances are they will return the favor. Acknowledgment is a powerful tool; wield it like a wand and tap on those you love.

Once you've become your own damn muse, you can keep yourself in good company by finding a couple of other muses out there that inspire you. Are there people in your community who are just so inspiring they make you want to do more? Is there someone in your office who challenges you in the best way? The practice of having a muse isn't about being obsessed with anyone in particular; it's about acknowledging the magical, sparkly things that other people emit and letting those things multiply within yourself. You never even need to speak to your muses to be inspired by them.

You can have different muses for different situations. My husband is my muse when it comes to work. I see the effort he puts into it. I see how committed he is to breaking stereotypes. He's not afraid to cry when he plays a legendary tough guy. He is generous with his affection. He cares very much about the words and will have hard conversations with writers and producers to make sure that the characters and stories are honored. Working with him on *The Walking Dead* was such a warm and fulfilling experience. We have very different relationships with acting. For me, it is something that I have done my entire life, having been put in classes while in preschool. Jeff came to it much later and struggled in Los Angeles for a lot of years before he started working. And so his appreciation for what he gets to do for a living is this beautiful reminder for me of what the work is really about.

My lifestyle muse is Susan Branch. She's an illustrator and writer whose cookbooks and gardening books became my obsession in my early twenties, when other girls were reading *Cosmo* and watching *Sex and the City*. I loved her brand of nostalgia, and

I wanted to build beautiful things at Mischief Farm in a way that paid respect to her.

My farming muses are the Beekman Boys. They didn't just farm for themselves; they took the opportunity to use their goat farm to support the economy of an entire small town here in New York. I can't tell you how much I love that way of thinking.

My writing muses are Alice Hoffman and the late, great Ray Bradbury. The way that Alice has written about women for decades is very important. She believes in imperfect women. She believes in the value of rebellion. She understands that sexuality is natural and not something for which a woman should be vilified. And she believes in the same kind of magic that I believe in. Her books offer me a safe retreat, and I want to make those same kinds of stories for other people.

My activism muse is Sophia Bush. She was on the ball helping other people while the rest of us were in our shitty twenties, thinking about ourselves and who we were going to kiss each weekend. Activism comes naturally to her, and she has a deep empathy for people she's never met before. Her boundless energy is baffling to me. I cannot conceive of having that much of myself to give away, and she does it effortlessly and with a great deal of style.

My parenting muse is my candy store business partner, Julie Rudd. I love her kids so much. And I love the family unit she created, because it gave me a template for how I could make my own family work in this weird, transient industry Jeffrey and I live in.

I've set up a little garden full of pedestals in my mind, holding up people like Alice and Sophia, Julie and Jeff, Susan and the Beekman Boys. They are people who make me want to be more. The people who make me want to go out there and take the world by storm, knowing I have powerful examples and inspirations to back me up.

Make Your Own
Oracle Deck

For every woman is at heart a witch.

—Charles Godfrey Leland, *Aradia, or the Gospel
of the Witches*

*A*n oracle deck is a collection of cards that offer you guidance through self-reflection. You could buy them, of course, and there are many lovely options to get you started. But a store-bought deck doesn't know who your personal heroes are. It couldn't possibly know what quotes or stories got you through that rough spot in tenth grade or through your painful divorce. A store-bought deck doesn't know the mixtape of your heart, and what lyrics you need to hear in moments of doubt.

But, if you *make* one, this will become a living journal of things that inspire you. I love that this creation is a lifelong project. I know that I'm not the only one to fall down a rabbit hole of curiosity, reading biographies and hunting down photos and tidbits of information on personalities that capture my attention. In high school, during the years I was obsessed with androgyny, Boy George was my hero. His face papered the walls of my bedroom, locker, and various book covers. In college, I fell for the salty humor of women like Ruth Gordon and Bea Arthur. During the tumultuous years of *One Tree Hill*, I'd sit at my kitchen table in the back of that haunted house and find comfort in the forceful voice of Nina Simone. I wanted a strength like that.

All of those versions of me still exist. They're floating around inside, waiting to be acknowledged. By creating a deck of my personal guides, I get to make the connection between who I *was* and what I *am* whenever I am in need of guidance.

Collect quotes, short stories, and pearls of wisdom that will inform you as you move through challenging days. Draw on your gods and goddesses, your grandparents, the people you most admire. Then, start crafting. Use sketches, collage, or postcards that you find. Create an evenly sized deck of cards with art on one side and wisdom on the other. Whenever you feel you need an external lift, or a new way of seeing a problem, your day, your life, shuffle the cards and draw one. Your oracle deck is an evolving project, as simple or ornate as you want. Even if you add only one new card a year, it is a catalogue of wisdom you can draw from whenever you need strength.

Here are some of my oracles. Notice many of them are writers or actors. Makes sense, because writing and acting are my two passions. Populate your own deck with voices that speak to your experience.

Ruth Gordon, actress and screenwriter

"The best impromptu speeches are the ones written well in advance."

The message: In other words, prepare, prepare, prepare.

Maxine Hong Kingston, novelist

"In a time of destruction, create something: a poem, a parade, a community, a school, a vow, a moral principle; one peaceful moment.

The message: The antidote to darkness is creation. Go bake a pie.

Gypsy Rose Lee, burlesque entertainer and writer

"It's not what you do. It's the way you do it—stripping, or writing, or talking . . . or just breathing. Do it with an air, and never admit you're scared."

The message: Fake it 'til you make it, babes.

Ray Bradbury, my favorite writer of all time

"If we listened to our intellect we'd never have a love affair. We'd never have a friendship. We'd never go in business because we'd be cynical . . . Well, that's nonsense. You're going to miss life. You've got to jump off the cliff all the time and build your wings on the way down."

The message: There is only reward in risk.

Carson McCullers, Southern Gothic writer

"I meditated on love and reasoned it out. I realized what is wrong with us. Men fall in love for the first time. And what do they fall in love with? . . . They fall in love with a woman. They start at the wrong end of love. They begin at the climax. Can you wonder it is so miserable? Do you know how men should love? A tree. A rock. A cloud."

The message: Focus on the beauty of small things right now.

Nina Simone, singer, songwriter, and activist

"You've got to learn to leave the table when love's no longer being served."

The message: Know the power of walking away.

Alice Hoffman, Queen Witch of novelists

"The moon is always jealous of the heat of the day, just as the sun always longs for something dark and deep."

The message: Find the beauty in both sides of the coin. It's natural to want both.

Gabriel García Márquez, novelist

"All human beings have three lives: public, private, and secret."

The message: Guard the different parts of you, and keep some things just for yourself.

Bea Arthur, actress

"I'm not playing a role. I'm being myself, whatever the hell that is."

The message: Stop pretending.

ENCHANTING
YOUR FOOD

he absolute easiest and most accessible way to add magic to your life is by realizing that you already create it multiple times a day. Through food, babes! Breakfast, lunch, dinner, tea, snacks—all present an opportunity to infuse real, honest-to-goodness magic in your life.

Many years ago, in an episode of Alton Brown's cooking show, I recall watching him explain that when you add spices to your food, it is very important that they come from your hand and not from the jar. The warmth of your hand can open up the spices in a way that brings them alive. They sit there dormant in a jar for how long before we use them? I liked that science backed up my more emotional instinct, and so now, I like to touch everything before I put it in the pot, part of my food magic. (Be a good grown-up and wash your hands, and encourage anyone else who's cooking with you to do the same!)

This kind of physicality can be applied to pretty much anything you want to cook. Are you seasoning meat? Use your hands to add that salt and pepper. Are you baking? Make intentions as you crack those eggs, even if you're just saying thank you to the creatures and plants you are using to make your meal.

When I make spaghetti sauce or chili, I make a point of having my son with me as we crush the whole Italian tomatoes in the pot by hand. I tell him to make a wish or an intention with each tomato he squeezes. I've been doing that for years. What my husband doesn't know is that sometimes when we've been bickering, I will do that as a little bit of love magic to calm him down. Crushing tomatoes becomes the action of quashing the argument. I don't know if it's the spell, or the fact that he feels really loved when he's cooked for . . . but that shit works! (Don't tell him!)

I DIDN'T COME FROM A MAGICAL FOOD HOUSEHOLD. THE ONLY ceremonies surrounding food were blowing out birthday candles. But as I grew up and started traveling, I wanted to collect all the cultural habits and practices I could. In Spain, you're supposed to eat twelve grapes at the stroke of midnight on New Year's Eve for good luck. In Miami, I was told that whenever you open a bottle of rum, you must pour out a few drops for the spirits. Bread and wine is transformed into the body and blood of Christ during communion. And how many of us are healed by the love put into grandma's chicken noodle soup?

One of my favorite books about cultural magic through the use of food is Mary-Grace Fahrun's *Italian Folk Magic*. I picked this book up right after my daughter was born and read it while I was nursing, and pumping and nursing, and pumping. My body was literally going through the magical process of making food, and I was fascinated by Fahrun's account of her Italian relatives using coffee, olive oil, and a slew of other ingredients to do things like ward off the evil eye or attract a lover. That was the kind of birthright magic that I craved. And similar to my lineage's practice of Appalachian magic that was decidedly Christian, Italian *nonnas* practice a devout form of Catholicism that honors God and calls upon the saints in everything from making soup to preparing their daily espresso.

Food is hereditary magic. In most cultures, the divine combination of ingredients and preparation ceremony turns everyday meals into a rewarding mystical experience. Cooking for people you care about is creating the ultimate love spell. I have collected cookbooks from every corner of this country. And I have always enjoyed poring over them with a cup of coffee or a pot of tea, learning new recipes as well as tinkering with those printed on the page.

During the pandemic, working in my kitchen—which was once a point of creativity and refuge—became a chore. I (like so many of us) was burnt-TF-out from cooking meals during those lockdown years. Preparing multiple meals a day for every member of our family felt like an insurmountable task, and given the limited supplies we had, a drudgery of repetition. I can make pasta only so many times. I could cook the root vegetables our local farm co-op delivered only a certain number of ways. My creativity was stifled and exhausted. It saddens me to say, but my great love for cooking was extinguished. I know I'm not the only one. The other mothers of my coven and I sent memes to each other lamenting the domestic chef's plot in life. Given that, how could I find the joy I'd once experienced as a kitchen witch? This is one of those very real situations where consulting my own grimoire gave me my magic back.

One of my favorite chapters of Ray Bradbury's *Dandelion Wine* describes his grandmother's kitchen. It is a storm of flour and salt and herbs and spices and biscuits and utensils and canisters and coffee, and it is the chaos of a life lived well. And in this story, an aunt comes to visit and decides to do grandma the great favor of tidying up and organizing her kitchen.

Grandma had never used recipes. She never measured ingredients. She just *felt* the food.

Suddenly, all the delicious dinners that had been created each evening with the mysticism of being a once-in-a-lifetime experience were gone. The meals made from the new, orderly kitchen were sterile, paste-like, and it wasn't until the aunt had been shipped off and the kitchen restored to its previous tumultuous glory that the joy of cooking and serving and eating was restored.

I REALLY FELT THAT STORY IN MY BONES. AS MUCH AS I LOVE cookbooks, what I love even more is *tinkering* with cookbooks. Because food is magic, and magic that you learn from someone else is certainly effective. But magic that you put your *own* stamp on is obviously going to be more powerful.

The jalapeño peppers I toss in from my own garden are going to make my Sweet Hot Pot Pie more powerful. The honey that comes from our local honey store, from bees who pollinate the fields that surround our own farm, is going to add a tangible magic.

Adding magical thought processes to your daily chores won't just make it better for the people you are taking care of; it is an act of great self-care. You deserve daily magic.

Sweet Hot Pot Pie

The kitchen, my kitchen, is the room where nourishing meals are prepared … It's where I go to pray. I meditate while I clean and pray while I cook. It is the room where most of my memories live. It is my temple, shrine, and altar.

—Mary-Grace Fahrun, *Italian Folk Magic:*
Rue's Kitchen Witchery

*P*utting together a pot pie is a work of improvisation. It's jazz.

Your mood will affect how much spice you add, how much honey, whether you dice the chicken with a knife or tear it with your bare hands. My husband understands he's being bewitched by my pie, and falls under its spell willingly. You, too, can be a pied piper. (See what I did there?)

INGREDIENTS:

Pie crust. Use your grammy's favorite recipe. Or if you're a shortcut lover like me, grab a package of crust at the grocery store. Either way, you'll need enough for a top and bottom crust.

Salt and pepper to taste

3 tsp turmeric (1 tsp for chicken, 2 tsp for stovetop pot)

6 chicken thighs

1/4 cup butter

2 medium yellow onions

2 peeled carrots, sliced into rounds on a veggie planer

4 ribs of celery chopped into 1/4-inch pieces

1/2 cup diced baby portobello mushrooms

1/2 cup diced red bell pepper

1 large chopped jalapeño pepper (the more seeds you keep, the spicier the filling)

2 tbsp minced garlic

1/3 cup flour

1/2 tsp ground sage

1 cup chicken stock

1/2 cup heavy cream

1/4 cup honey

1 tsp crushed red pepper

1/4 cup frozen peas

INSTRUCTIONS:

Preheat the oven to 450 degrees F.

Line a baking sheet with parchment paper. Sprinkle the lined sheet with a hefty pinch of salt, pepper, and the 1 teaspoon of turmeric. Pat your chicken thighs down with paper towel and roll them in the spices. (This is a good point to press any intentions into your main ingredient. Turmeric is anti-inflammatory, so this is the perfect meal to quash problems!)

Put the chicken in the oven and bake for 15–20 minutes, until juices run clear.

Meanwhile, in a large pot, melt the butter over medium heat. Add in the onions first, dashing them with a pinch of salt so they sweat and get sweet. Stir as they cook, for about 5 minutes.

Add the carrots and celery, and stir for 5 minutes more.

While that is happening, dice the mushrooms and bell peppers.

Pull the chicken from the oven once it is done and let it cool so that it's easy to handle.

Add the bell and jalapeño peppers to the pot and continue to stir as they soften a bit.

Add the mushrooms and garlic, and cook for 2 minutes.

Once all the vegetables have been added, coat them in the flour and stir continuously for 2 minutes, so that everything is coated.

Pour in the chicken stock and heavy cream, and then add the remaining turmeric and the sage. Raise the heat to medium high.

Add in the honey and the crushed red pepper, representing the duality of love: sweetness and fire.

Once the chicken can be handled, either cut it into ½-inch pieces or tear it by hand as you recite intentions. If you do this during a waning moon, it's a powerful way to break bad habits, quit toxic relationships, and end cycles that are no longer working for you. Add the chicken to the pot.

Let simmer for 10 minutes so all the flavors begin to play nice. Then, right before you add your filling to the pie shell, toss in the frozen peas. Make wishes on them if you're moved to do so.

Line your pie pan with dough, add the filling, and then top with another sheet of dough, crimping the crust all the way along the edges. Once sealed up, you'll need to cut vents in the top of the pie. You can carve initials, symbols, or whatever you like.

Put the pie pan on a baking sheet so that your oven doesn't get messy if the pie bubbles over, and place in the oven for 15 minutes. Do a check at that point to make sure your crust isn't burning. If it is golden brown, toss a sheet of aluminum foil over the pie and cook for 5 more minutes.

Let the pie rest for 5 minutes before slicing up and serving.

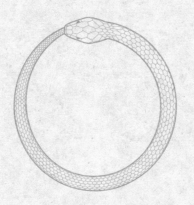

GIVING IT AWAY

 grimoire can be anything. Truly. It can be a garden like Mr. Stillman's, riddled with symbolism and deep feelings. It can be a steamer trunk full of paintings and treasures from your travels, much like the inheritance Elisabeth Chant left Hester Donnelly. It can be the modern-day catalogue of knowledge that Mr. Johnson created on his Facebook page, recorded for all posterity. At its core, the grimoire is the accumulated collection of love and hard work and inspiration. It is the gift we give to the people we love, that they can share with the people they love, and so on and so forth until the ripple effects of our existence pass far beyond our personal scope.

While I was in the process of writing *The Rural Diaries*, I was producing a movie down in Louisiana. It was a strange experience, to pore over pages that chronicled the journey I had been on with friends and loved ones, and then go onto set where I'd had the good fortune of *casting* a number of those friends and loved ones. Tyler Hilton and Megan Park were along for the ride. My neighbor Bruce MacVittie was playing my father. Old friends from *One Tree Hill*—Lee Norris, Colin Fickes, Barbara Alyn Woods, Antwon Tanner, and Rhoda Griffis—came aboard. But with a tight budget and an even tighter schedule, I needed to figure out a local hire in Louisiana to play my boss. Wouldn't you know it, my old sweetheart from my days on *White Collar*, Willie Garson, had recently bought a fabulous historic home in New Orleans!

My relationship with Willie was always difficult for me to explain. It was instant. It was a safe space where I felt confident. It was cemented in a no-bullshit policy that meant we told each other the truth, even when it was hard. It was loving and tender, and I cherished being the gal on his arm. To be one of Willie's girls was a badge of honor. He had no time for shrinking violets and liked to playfully spar with smart, brassy broads. He tackled the world the way I did. The need to soak up as much as humanly possible ran deeply in both of us. Sometimes it's just easy to spot one of your own kind.

I texted and asked him if he would come to play on the movie, knowing full well he would say yes. No one loved being on set more than Willie Garson. He arrived within days and set to work charming everyone, elevating the material and lavishing me with stories about his new chapter in New Orleans. He'd been a lifelong lover of the city and its restaurants, cultural landmarks, and Jazz Fest. It was a bawdy town for a bawdy man, and I loved both. I was blatantly using work as an opportunity to catch up with one of my favorite humans, so Willie and I would sneak off to my trailer, where we'd gossip about mutual friends or who his son Nathen, a high school senior at the time, was kissing. He saw that I was exhausted, and I walked him through the process of writing the book and the edits and the photo shoot that was being planned for as soon as I got home.

"Well, if you can write a book, I can write a book!" he said. And I knew it to be true! Willie had been in the business for decades, working on major network comedies and dramas since 1986. He had an idea for how to structure his own biography. As a teenager in the 1970s, he'd found a naughty book in his father's bedroom dresser. *My First 500* was the sexual autobiography of an actress named Rachel English, and it focused on exactly what it sounds like: her first five hundred sexual partners. I was belly laughing as Willie expressed the exhilaration of finding this sordid piece of art. English recounted every lover she ever had, giving some of them long-winded romantic narratives, while others received a sentence, possibly two. "So, I'm just gonna apply this method to my career," Willie explained. "I'll go through credit by credit and it'll be my entire adult life." It was a smart plan! Willie had been in about 170 different shows and movies, sometimes doing guest spots, but other times performing years' worth of content as beloved colorful characters. Dedicating a few paragraphs to each job would be a fun recounting of not only his life, but American pop culture.

After we wrapped the movie, Willie went back to New Orleans and I went home to New York. I saw him a couple of months later at my wedding. He was seated on the aisle, and his beaming face was one of the first I saw as I entered the ceremony. Willie had known Jeff for decades, as they'd done a failed television pilot back in the 1980s. He was such a presence that evening, and at the night's end he snapped what would become Jeff's favorite picture of me. Standing across from the tattoo booth we had set up at the reception, Willie watched as I got my Mischief tattoo inked across my forearm. I'd danced and sweat my lashes off and my hair was stuck to my face. I was an absolute mess! But Willie shouted over the music, "Hil! Look up!" and with his phone he captured a sloppy, blissfully happy, girlish version of me that he had absolutely contributed to creating.

In January, he'd send us a wedding gift, *The Grapes of Wrath*, along with a loving handwritten note. (A book *and* paper mail?! My friend knew me well.)

> *First edition, first printing (the book jacket is a reproduction of the original, mint ones are like $15,000—I mean I like you, but calm down.)*
> *The only book that really matters in my opinion. About honor, and decency and a bumpy ride and family—everything that the two of you represent to so many of us, both together and individually.*

The pandemic would strike soon after that, and Willie and I would team up for multiple Zoom charity events, our banter and obvious love for each other an easy thing to share with the wider world. We hadn't fully emerged from our isolation in the summer of 2021, but Willie had secured a significant story line in the *Sex and the City* limited series that was filming in New York. He'd gotten an apartment for Nathen and himself right down the street from our place, and texts flew back and forth about how we were finally going to escape lockdown and get back to the business of living. Going to dinner with Willie was one of my greatest joys while filming *White Collar,* and he introduced me to a whole new world of Manhattan hot spots and secret foodie delights. He made the city seem like something out of an old movie, another shared affinity we had. He would send texts like:

Watching this old movie on TCM "All Fall Down" and you literally ARE Eva Marie Saint, like LITERALLY

In August 2021, I was spread impossibly thin. I'd taken on too many jobs, had to empty out the entire house into storage containers for repairs while writing lesson plans for Gus's home-schooling, and I was undeniably raw from Markie's passing. I'd taken up corresponding with her magical daughters Daisy and Kate, talking fairies and flowers. Just like the garden, something new was blooming in the wake of loss.

But just ten days after I'd gotten the news about her, my phone pinged. I had an email. From Willie. My immediate reaction was, *What charity are we doing now?* I just assumed we'd meet up in the city and try to do some good and then hit one of the restaurants he'd discovered on this latest trip to the east coast. But Willie wasn't in New York anymore.

"*I love you,*" the message said.

It was a mass letter, sent to an unknown number of recipients.

DO NOT FALL APART. You're gonna do what you have to do, and I get that ... The time has come to tell people that I've been battling pancreatic cancer since September 2020. My focus has been on hopeful treatment, and taking care of Nathen. ... I ask for privacy. ... Please ask people to avoid picking up the phone to call me immediately. I feel your love, I know your love. All of my friends are my best friends, and that's why they are my friends to begin with.

I don't want to write about what I felt or how I reacted. It was—and is—agonizing. Willie Garson was a proud man, and I knew he was serious when he said he didn't want to turn into a sideshow. So, I sent a gentle message, along with a childhood picture of him that I held dear.

"Don't respond. Just a flare to say that I love this little animal a great deal."

There was a flurry of communication between his various overlapping circles. Our *White Collar* family was in constant contact. Our castmate Tim DeKay had been one of the very few people who had known about Willie's illness. Tim is a man of integrity and grace, and even in the midst of his own grief, he counseled each of us with great care, so that we would have answers without having to pester Willie or his family.

Willie was still posting on social media, giving no indication that anything was wrong. It was business as usual. But I hadn't heard back from him. It felt like a damned-if-you-do, damned-if-you-don't situation. I wanted to respect his wishes, but it was killing me. He'd told Tim that deathbed visits only benefited the living, not the dying. Why make more work for him when he was in pain? On August 24, there was an opening. I'd posted a picture of all of us girls from *One Tree Hill* on my Instagram. He commented privately on the photo. I took the opportunity to pounce:

"Listen, Mister. It is taking every cell in my body to not smother you with attention. I love you."

There was a back-and-forth. That conversation is mine. But the last missive of the evening was a video I sent him, a 1967 performance of Lulu singing "To Sir, with Love."

A friend who taught me right from wrong
And weak from strong
That's a lot to learn.
What, what can I give you in return?
If you wanted the sky
I would write across the sky in letters
That would soar a thousand feet high,
"To Sir, with love."

The next morning there was an email in my inbox. The subject line said, "Don't freak out." It was addressed to me, Willie's brother-in-law Jerry, and his longtime representative, Chris.

Promise me. Please. I know I'm loved. Deeply, by you. And it's right back at you.

This is for Hilarie, but have copied Chris Schmidt and Jerry Levine, who can help if any discussions are needed.

It was Willie's book.

His entire life, job by job, chapter by chapter, strung like colorful beads on a Mardi Gras necklace.

There is an insecurity that death brings out for those who are left behind. *Did they love me as much as I loved them? Was it real?* I am always afraid that I'm being too dramatic, or that my emotions are embarrassing for other people. I'd felt that in the days I hadn't heard from Willie. But maybe he had, too. He needed to know what a giant he was in my life. And by sending me his book and entrusting me with putting it out into the world, he gave me the security that it *was* real: the love, the friendship, the trust.

I needed to see him. Right away. I booked a flight for the next day and scrambled to get childcare and the farm in order so I could be gone. Like a chicken with its head cut off, I busied myself, and then panicked in the afternoon with the thought, *How can I show him that he means the world to me?* Words fall flat, especially among actors. We spend our whole lives delivering scripted dialogue and practicing intense scenes. I wanted my sentiments to transcend that. The only way I could think to do that was to create something permanent. I already had tattoos on me for people I'd lost whom I had really cared about, like my friend Scott, who died in Iraq. But it was important to me to have this symbol before Willie passed so that *he* would know it was there. I wanted the tattoo in a place that was visible so that I could talk about him to people. I sat in my car and made some impulsive phone calls to local tattoo parlors, and the folks at Hudson Valley Tattoo Company were incredibly sympathetic to my situation. They brought me in and sneaked me off into a corner where an artist named Hiten Damodar had me sit down. I'd brought the letter that Willie had sent along with our wedding gift. "Can you put this on my forearm?" I asked. This stranger was kind and calm as he began the process of copying Willie's handwriting. "Calm down" would be a mantra I would carry with me forever.

The next day, I was at Willie's bedside. Tim DeKay and his wife, Elisa, were a lifeline, dropping me off at Willie's house, sharing in the storytelling, and making sure I ate. I'd decided to dress up to see Willie. It must have been an odd sight for his family, this strange woman showing up in a dress and full hair and makeup. But Willie loved dames. Willie's brother John and Jerry led me back to his room. The moment I entered the doorway, my guy had a big smile. "Whoa," he said. "You did yourself up!"

I leaned in and kissed his head. "I wore the lowest-cut dress I own, pal." Willie laughed.

"Oh good, me too," he said, pulling down on his hospital gown. We played catch-up like it was a totally normal hangout, ignoring the impossible elephant in the room. We talked about our kids, about the traveling we'd both done in the last year, and about his favorite subject: work. And I told him that Jeffrey and I were going into the liquor business. Willie lit up. "Bring me my laptop," he said.

Simple tasks had become difficult. And so, it was somber to witness my razor-sharp friend navigate slowly as he searched for a document and sent it to my email. It was a comprehensive list of every restaurant, every bar, and every historic must-see in New Orleans, and he was adamant that I have it. "You can't have a liquor company and not be in New Orleans."

Over the course of the visit, I would catch Willie looking at his words on my arm. It's important to let people know, while we still have them, what they mean to us. I wanted him to be a part of my forever story. We laughed. We reminisced. We talked shit. His nephews and nieces and cousins and siblings came in and we took turns orbiting around him. He'd told me he was sick of questions about food and bodily functions. "You want me to go get *My First 500*?" I'd asked.

"Yes!" Of course he did. The nieces and nephews and I had a ball with the excerpts, and the suggestive description on the back cover. We talked about Willie's book and discussed the ways in which I wanted to include his friends in the final product. I held his hand and tried to absorb every little detail. The signet ring that he always wore. The piercing blue of his eyes. The way he touched his chest when he talked.

It was a good visit.

I came out a week later for Markie's memorial and another good visit with Willie. But it was harder than the last. We were losing him. Before I left, I stood at his bedroom door in front of his remaining friends and family. I locked eyes with him. "I love you," I said, firmly. He knew.

ANOTHER TRIP TO LA WAS SCHEDULED FOR TEN DAYS LATER. BEFORE I could see him again, Willie slipped away on September 21.

I had blocked off time to be with him before I got the news. And so rather than go sit at my cherished friend's bedside, I went to Jerry's house to sit shiva with his family. There was Nathen, wearing his father's signet ring, a talisman to keep Willie close. There were so many of the friends and relatives I'd met over the previous month. There were coworkers that I'd only read about in Willie's book. And there was our *White Collar* family, Marsha Thomason and Sharif Atkins, faces I had missed so much. We talked and talked and talked about Willie's book. And it seemed a number of us had received the legendary New Orleans guide.

Without even intending to, Willie had left us a grimoire. He had collected his knowledge, his experiences, his favorite things, and he bundled them up so that we could feel his love. It was an inheritance.

I went home. I went to work. I lived and loved and tried to make sense of this messy journey. I wrote everything down—obviously—and I began piecing this grimoire of my own together. It had lived in scraps and chunks of different notebooks and journals. How to order things? How do they all fit together?

And it does all fit together. As I neared completion, Tara had a proposal for me: "A new section of the garden has been uncovered. It's called The Little Wilderness. Toshi and our new gardener, Alaina, are restoring it to what it once was and we need funding, but I think you should come see the statuary."

Two long-forgotten statues had been uncovered in the glade of the nymphs, right near the house at Wethersfield. *How did we miss these?* I wondered. One was a regal nymph, lined up within eyesight of the Diana and Hippolytus statues. Near her was an elaborate fountain that looked like the ruins of an ancient temple column. Paperwork from the estate suggested it was Egeria. I'd known nothing about this myth, and so dove into research.

Not just any nymph, Egeria played an important role in the mythology of the Romans as the divine partner to Numa Pompilius, the second king of Rome. He claimed that she counseled him nightly in all of his dealings within the city, and he was said to have written down her lessons in sacred books that were buried with him. Egeria was the liaison between King Numa and the Muses. Under her guidance, the king established the council of Vestal Virgins—a group of six priestesses—and led Rome away from its inclination to war and toward peace.

In 673 BC, King Numa died, sending Egeria into a fit of despair. She wailed and wept in the woods near the shrine of Diana, and the other nymphs, who at first felt pity for her, grew weary. They begged her to stop and then petitioned Hippolytus to intervene. He shared his own stories of grief with her, but Egeria continued to weep. Hippolytus turned to his goddess Diana. *What could be done?* Diana understood that denying grief wasn't the answer. And so, she turned Egeria into a pool of water so that she could weep forever.

I needed this part of the garden to exist. Chauncey Stillman never knew me. He died when I was a child. He had no idea that a curious friend of his granddaughter's would come along one day and find the comfort she so desperately needed in the antiquity of his garden grimoire. "I want to fund this," I told Tara. And so, trails were mulched and brush was cleared and poison ivy was removed by the truckload. Plants were purchased, and a plan for an ethereal doorway made of branches was created by Alaina. A new tree was being planted in The Little Wilderness. There would be a small brass plaque, a tribute to Willie and all the loved ones we mourned along the great path.

Much had been lost, but much had also been gained.

Who was I without the loving mentorship of Bruce Johnson? Who was Hester without the eccentric Elisabeth Chant in her life? Who was Tara without the sensitive and creative message her grandfather Chauncey Stillman left for her to decode? Who was Dante without the guidance of Virgil to lead him through the Dark Wood?

There is a ripple effect to true magic. Drop a pebble in the water and you will see the rings of impact expand and multiply. That is what we are doing here. Each spell, each intention, each action is the dropped pebble. We can't control who or what our ripple effects will touch, but we know that the circles of love and inheritance are one and the same. And so, if we are lucky, we absorb the impact left by others, collect it in our own personal grimoires with enthusiasm and good intentions, and then drop it when our time is over, sending brand-new rings of magic out into the world.

Ithaka

Ithaka

by C. P. CAVAFY

Translated by Edmund Keeley

As you set out for Ithaka
hope your road is a long one,
full of adventure, full of discovery.
Laistrygonians, Cyclops,
angry Poseidon—don't be afraid of them:
you'll never find things like that on your way
as long as you keep your thoughts raised high,
as long as a rare excitement
stirs your spirit and your body.
Laistrygonians, Cyclops,
wild Poseidon—you won't encounter them
unless you bring them along inside your soul,
unless your soul sets them up in front of you.

Hope your road is a long one.
May there be many summer mornings when,

with what pleasure, what joy,
you enter harbors you're seeing for the first time;
may you stop at Phoenician trading stations
to buy fine things,
mother of pearl and coral, amber and ebony,
sensual perfume of every kind—
as many sensual perfumes as you can;
and may you visit many Egyptian cities
to learn and go on learning from their scholars.

Keep Ithaka always in your mind.
Arriving there is what you're destined for.
But don't hurry the journey at all.
Better if it lasts for years,
so you're old by the time you reach the island,
wealthy with all you've gained on the way,
not expecting Ithaka to make you rich.

Ithaka gave you the marvelous journey.
Without her you wouldn't have set out.
She has nothing left to give you now.

And if you find her poor, Ithaka won't have fooled you.
Wise as you will have become, so full of experience,
you'll have understood by then what these Ithakas mean.

AFTERWORD

As I was finishing up final edits, my husband and I attended the memorial for our dear friend Bruce MacVittie. He had played my dad in the same Christmas movie Willie had joined and had been a trusted friend to grieve with after Willie passed. Bruce left behind a doting army of friends, and we were doing our best to show up for his amazing wife, Carol, and daughter, Sophie. Prayer cards were passed out, and Bruce's love for all of us was suddenly tangible. Rather than place a quote or a religious verse on a single card, it was a little palm-sized booklet. The very cherished recipe for Bruce's famous Sunday sauce was now in all of our hands. He'd made pasta dinner for our family countless times, always tweaking the recipe to thoughtfully account for our kids' dietary restrictions and feeding Jeffrey whenever he was alone in the city for work. Bruce was so good and generous that way. I had just finished the chapters on "Enchanting Your Food" and "Giving It Away" and here was our very missed friend modeling both sentiments with a mini grimoire that shared his proud Italian heritage and widespread love for his family and friends. Everyone talked about how meaningful it was.

I came home and placed it in my own grimoire.

I wrapped this book up and headed into the holiday season, fully aware that the stories I began here were still unfolding.

Park View High School had gotten word that the school board approved a minuscule budget for renovations. It wasn't even close to being able to tackle the water leaks and asbestos and dated infrastructure of the tired building. But this time, there was a chorus of voices, led by PTSA President Amy Gazes.

"No more!" everyone shouted. We were collectively tired of these kids getting the scraps. And the voices were too loud to ignore this time. The school board revised their plan, and the kids of Sterling Park will soon have a *brand-new* building, with all the bells and whistles the other kids in the county enjoy. A part of my own personal Ithaca will be destroyed to make way for something better. It's bittersweet. But my home was never the actual cinderblocks or the wooden bleachers or the stage where I'd found myself at eight years old. It was those people. The teachers and lifelong classmates. The new sea of hopeful teenagers who throw outrageous pep rallies. In them, Ithaca lives.

That news felt like the perfect update to end the book.

But then life, as it does, came back swinging.

On December 18, 2022, I woke up with a text alert on my phone. I saw Rabbi George's name and was excited to exchange holiday pleasantries and photos and tell him the book was finally all done and turned in. Only it wasn't George. *Hilarie, this is George's sister Lin. George was admitted to the local hospital 12/11 and declined rapidly.*

No.

My sweet neighbor had passed the day before. I was shocked, and so grateful to his sister for even thinking to tell me. Rabbi George had just re-entered my life. It felt like a huge cheat to lose him so abruptly. He was supposed to come visit the farm. I was gonna come help him organize his house so he could downsize.

I wrote back and thanked Lin and tried to find the words to explain to her that I thought the world of her brother. That reuniting with him over ghost stories for this book was so much more to me than just storytelling. It was an act of bearing witness to each other's lives. She responded to me:

"He loved being able to defend, protect and enjoy your personality as you were becoming you. He proudly showed me photos of your children. George was so pleased with your marriage and children. He felt you were safe and happy. Just like a father would be."

The grace it takes to reach out to a stranger in your own moment of grief is incredible. My heart broke over losing Rabbi George, but I also felt deep gratitude for his sister. I am so glad I got writer's block and had to push my deadlines. I am so glad that Rabbi George butt-dialed me. I am so glad that we got to gossip and catch up for hours and hours. I am so glad this book gave me the chance to interview him and thank him for what he meant to me as a twenty-one year old. He is imprinted on my grimoire forever, and his joy and energy and love of gardening are things I will pass along to Gus and my daughter George. Is it any wonder that I wanted to give her a name that I held with so much affection and respect?

AND SO, THE GRIMOIRE CONTINUES TO WRITE ITSELF. THERE ARE deaths and losses where we collect what we can as a final act of love. And there are births and rebirths that we fight for and celebrate. My sincere hope for you, dear reader, is that you create something that holds all your loves, all your knowledge, and all your magic and that it fills your cup and feeds your life. That it protects you and reminds you how absolutely incredible you are. And when you are ready, I hope that you pass that inheritance along, filling up other cups and leaving mischief in your wake.

ACKNOWLEDGMENTS

This book was written over the course of a couple of rough years, and so I hope the entirety of it exists as an acknowledgement of gratitude for every person mentioned.

Meg Mortimer, my constant rock. You are my family.

Liz DeCesare, my work wife. You've made so many of my dreams into realities.

Jordan Manekin, you absolute smoke show. You make me feel safe.

Steve Pregiato and Catherine Hughes. Thank you for managing all my chaos!

Anthony Mattero and Yuni Sher and the rest of the gang at CAA, how did I get so lucky? Thank you for seeing me.

Barry McPherson, I appreciate you so much, sweet man.

Katy Hamilton and the HarperOne family, thank you for your unconditional support as I continue to grow.

Alexis Gargagliano, my teacher!!! Medusa is everywhere!

Dad. Thank you for the imagination.

My Work Families—MTV, *OTH*, the Christmas gang, Samuel's Sweet Shop, *Friday Night In*, AMC/Sundance, *Drama Queens*, our iHeart team, Bungalow, *It Couldn't Happen Here* crew—this list is endless, but my huge thank-you to all of you for helping me spin *all* the plates, usually at the exact same time.

My towns—Sterling Park, Wilmington, NYC, and Rhinebeck. You are warm and safe and I love you.

Park View—Go Patriots!

Every teacher I've ever had, I'll see you dames in the next book club meeting! And I'll probably cry again. Thank you for being so big in my life.

Mrs. Johnson, you and Bruce saw me before I saw me. I'm so proud to be one of yours.

Nathen, John and Karen, Jerry and Nina, Willie's loved ones and the *White Collar* family—I miss him so much. He collected the best people. Let's just keep telling his stories. XO

Daisy and Kate and Michael. Your Markie stole all of our hearts and made us believe in magic. I love you.

Carol and Sophie, laughter and wine and late-night rooftops visits. We Morgans are happy that we get to be with you for all of it.

Lin, your brother George was a true gentleman. I'm thankful for him, and for your kindness.

My Covens (past, present and future), Squatches, Slyphs, Pink Ladies, etc.—if you're mentioned in here it is because I love you and miss you when we are apart and writing about you gives me a chance to visit you and the memories.

Gus Morgan. You are the most exciting person I've ever met. I love how empathetic you are, how thoughtful you are, and how you make it all look easy. You are magic, my Gus. The creativity and light just pour out of you. Your gifts are endless.

George Morgan. You are the most powerful person I've ever met. You are dreams come true. I hope you always know how much I respect and adore you. No one is quicker with a joke or a well-timed hug, and your cleverness is only exceeded by your capacity for love. My animal whisperer, you enchant everyone and everything.

Jeffrey, my Jeffrey, oh Jeffrey. Remember right when we met, how scared you got when I started talking about witches? Riding fireballs across the desert! I realize that in our time together, I have been so many different versions of myself. Thank you for supporting each of them. Thank you for knowing how important curiosity is to me. Thank you for holding me during those really dark days. Thank you for knowing when to give space or cling tight. I love your face and your voice and the way you sleep at the beach and navigate the city and make fires at the farm and love our children with wild abandon. Mischief.